# The Dream of Bath

*A graphic portrait of her heritage and people*

With text by Diana Winsor

**Trade & Travel Publications Limited**
Parsonage Lane, Bath, England
MCMLXXX

© 1980   Trade & Travel Publications Limited

Printed by Dawson & Goodall Limited
The Mendip Press, Parsonage Lane, Bath

Paper: Highland Art, supplied by James McNaughton, Bristol
Lithographic plates by Aldercolour, Poole
Bound by Leighton-Straker, London

Designed by Robert Axten

ISBN 0 900751 16 9

Trade & Travel Publications Limited
Parsonage Lane, Bath BA1 1EN
Tel: Bath 64156 (STD Code 0225) Telex: 444756 SAMBOK G

# Contents

CAVENDISH PLACE, LANSDOWN CRESCENT &c. BATH.

# *Acknowledgments*

BATH is a photographer's delight, and never more so than now, when so much of the stone has been cleaned. Most of the pictures in this book are the work of contemporary photographers; others, culled from many sources, include several which have not been reproduced in book form before. We gratefully acknowledge the gracious permission of Her Majesty the Queen to reproduce from the Royal Collection a china medallion depicting the Coronation of King Edgar at Bath Abbey.

We wish to record our debt to Miss Jill Knight of the Bath Art Gallery, who helped us to locate and photograph many unique items from the City's archives. The administration of The Pump Room, Bath Reference Library, Bath Museums Service, the Royal National Hospital for Rheumatic Diseases, the American Museum, the Holburne of Menstrie Museum, the Photographic Department of the University of Bath, and the Trustees of Bath's Theatre Royal, all gave valuable assistance, and we are most grateful to them.

Similar help was given by local firms including Stothert & Pitt, Rotork Engineering, Horstmanns, the Bath & Portland Group, Sparrows, The Pitman Press, and the *Bath & Wilts Evening Chronicle* (Wessex Newspapers). *The Dream of Bath* is enhanced by the inclusion of some important pictures reproduced by permission of The National Portrait Gallery, The Governors of Dulwich Picture Gallery, The B.B.C. Hulton Picture Library, and The Geological Society of London.

The photographs are the work of Dr. Leslie Bowcock, M.B., Ch.B., A.I.M.B.I., A.R.P.S., President-Elect of The Royal Photographic Society, Frans Vahrmeyer, A.M.P.A. and Heather Vahrmeyer, A.M.P.A., of Unichrome, Graham Harrison and John Betteridge. An itemized list of the illustrations appears at the end of the book.

We acknowledge with gratitude the practical encouragement given by those who supported this publishing venture in purchasing the special limited edition.

# Panegyric

Of all the gay places the world can afford,
By gentle and simple for pastime ador'd,
Fine balls and fine concerts, fine buildings and springs,
Fine walks and fine views, and a thousand fine things,
(Not to mention the sweet situation and air),
What place, my dear mother, with Bath can compare?

Christopher Anstey
*The New Bath Guide* (1766)

# Introduction

Everybody knows Bath. Hot springs, and Georgian architecture, Bath Buns and Roman Baths. "A Queen enchanted", the poet Swinburne called it: "England's Florence".

But do we really know Bath? Why was this Italianate confection of honey-coloured stone first built here in a damp Somerset valley? Who were the men who built it, homesick for the comforts of Rome? And how strange that more than 1,500 years later, an obsessive young architect should recreate his own dream of Aquae Sulis here in what had become an undistinguished mediaeval town. Why Bath? Who were the people who lived and worked here and made it into one of the most beautiful cities of Europe? What of Bath today?

The answers are in this new book, *The Dream of Bath*. It tells the story of the city which for almost 2,000 years has occupied a unique place in the life of Britain. Since the people of the Celtic tribe of the Dobunni first called the hot springs the Waters of Sul, Bath has reflected the dreams, the hopes—the human weakness and frivolity of contemporary society. In every age men and women have come here to find solace for something, whether boredom, gout, penury or spinsterhood; at Bath was the chance to sample a taste of Pompeii, to find a rich heiress or build a perfect Palladian crescent on a hill. And out of this disorderly mixture of human motives has emerged a city of unparalleled charm, appreciated today as perhaps never before.

(Below) Old Bath Stone mine workings
known as 'The Cathedral', so high were
the pillars of limestone. (1B)

# Fleshpots of Siberia

It is formed of three elements. The first
is stone. The second, water: the third,
man. If ever there was a monument to
humanity's weakness, hypochondria and
frivolity, it is the city of Bath. It was
built in the beginning upon the dreams
of men who hungered for Rome, and
the sun on the stone of Lepcis Magna.
Men who found in this damp valley, on
a twist of an unreliable Celtic river, an
unbelievable commodity: hot water. So
Aquae Sulis refreshed the men of the
legions, and Bath today remains a
continuing refreshment to the eye and
the spirit.

But first, there was the stone. A white
limestone, part of the great Jurassic
beds of Britain that run from Portland
in Dorset north to the Yorkshire moors.
It is called freestone, for it may be cut
in any direction, but it must be laid
within a building the same way up as it
lay within the earth, for so it was
formed some 150 million years ago
when great seas moved over the
fragmenting continents of the globe.
Grains of calcareous shell and fossil in
the sediments of the shifting oceans,
grains of sand, became coated with lime
in the subterranean currents. Under the
microscope you can sometimes see tiny
shells at the heart of the individual
grains in the stone. Such grains are
called ooliths. Bath Stone is, technically,
an oolitic limestone. When first cut, it is
pale, then turning pale honey colour. In
*Persuasion,* Jane Austen writes of "the
white glare of Bath".

In 1819, Peter Egan described a visit
to the stone quarries at Combe Down in
his *Walks Around Bath*:

"The lofty arches, or pillars,
remaining in a craggy state, left by the
excavators to let in light to the
subterraneous passages and caverns
which extend for a considerable way
under the earth, most interestingly claim
the attention of the explorer. The Great
Oolite is deposited in thick beds, and
separated into vast blocks by vertical
fissures, the sides of which are
frequently embossed by the most
delicate stalactites, and beautiful spars of
diversified crystallization."

From such fissures in the rock came the water. No one knows how long ago it spilled from the earth, but it was probably more than 100,000 years. The water we see today is now known to have fallen as rain some 10,000 years ago, seeping down to rock stratas thousands of feet below the surface. Its flow appears to remain constant: the most recent measurement in 1979 showed that the King's Spring produces 288,000 gallons a day, and the smaller Hetling Spring is thought to yield about 24,000. Certainly there is no infiltration into the water, even after heavy rains—the water that emerges does not vary at all in flow or composition. Where it first bubbled forth in the valley, the ground never froze, although the woods that enfolded it like a bear's pelt might be white with snow. It steamed like the wild deer's breath, for it flowed at a temperature of about 120 degrees Farenheit (domestic hot water is around 140 degrees). It stained the mud red with iron oxide, and smelled of

sulphur. No wonder that the Celtic peoples who lived on the high green hills above the valley of the mists called it sacred, and believed that in the place of the hot springs dwelt the goddess Sul.

On those green hills surrounding the valley were other springs, cool clear water. They were a natural place for the peoples of the Iron Age to settle some 500 years BC, and the shape of one of their fortified settlements can still be seen on the round green summit of Little Solsbury Hill, north of the London Road. Bath is set in a bowl of seven hills—like Rome—which local people call downs: Combe Down, Claverton, Bathampton, Bannerdown, Lansdown, Southdown, Odd Down. Many must have been inhabited before the Romans, when the dark native peoples of Britain had mingled with the Celts moving west and north. They marked their lives by the seasons, birth and death, the feasts of Beltane, Samain, Lammas. They were not a people of the sun. Julius Caesar said of

the Celts that they measured time not in days, but in nights.

One of those early people, so local legend says, was a young prince of the west country whose father Hudibras banished him from court in about 500 BC because he suffered from a kind of leprosy. Condemned to wander alone, Prince Bladud lived by tending a herd of pigs, but found that they too began to suffer from his own sores. Yet when they came to the place in the valley that never froze, and wallowed in the warm mud, though he chased them out he found that the lesions on their black bristled skins were healing. He, too, bathed in the hot springs. And he was cured. He returned to his father's court, and when he became king, Bath became a sacred place of healing.

The royal line of Bladud did not endure, although his son was Shakespeare's King Lear. But there may be truth in the old legend. Pigs and men do have an affinity that predisposes them to similar diseases and their skins

(Opposite) The original Roman relieving arch of the outfall drain on the edge of the Roman reservoir. (5)

(Right) The original Roman main drain from the Roman Baths. (3)

are equally affected by deficiencies of certain trace elements—zinc, for instance, which makes them susceptible to such ailments as ringworm, mange, and the sores of pityriasis. Minute quantities of zinc are found in the hot springs. Long after Bladud's cure, a consulting physician on the Bath Waters called J. G. Douglas Kerr—one of many such at the end of the 19th century—wrote thus:

"In a case recently sent me, where there were few patches as large as a crown piece over the whole body free from Psoriasis, the patient rapidly improved after a fortnight's bathing and left with nearly a clean skin. This case was double interesting, as the baths of many continental spas had been tried in vain."

The medical profession is more sceptical today, although scientific analysis has shown the waters to contain some 30 different minerals and various elements including calcium, magnesium, lead, potassium, iron, lithium and sulphur. It is also slightly radioactive, and about three times as hard as normally hard water since it contains so much dissolved lime. But Arthur Braxtone, one of the City workmen whose domain is that subterranean world under the vaulted pavements of Bath, where you stumble on Roman masonry and medieval and Georgian conduits, believes in it:

"Many's the time I've been stiff and weary and felt the hot water lap around me and melt the little crystalline bits in my muscles, and I've never felt so good. Maybe it's all in the mind, but then, the mind's the most important bit of you, isn't it? You can't use the water for central heating and that because it's terrible hard and scales the pipes—but who are we to ignore all that water coming hot and free out of the earth?"

Which was precisely what the Romans thought. When Emperor

(Right) The Diving Stone – the Great Bath. (4)

Claudius invaded Britain in AD 43, almost 100 years after Caesar first landed and called the Celtic tribes the Britanni, it was not long before not only he but his legions realised that this was not, as had been thought, an island of gold. Boadicea nearly put an end to the whole occupation when she led a revolt against Rome and killed 70,000 people, according to Tacitus, including every man of the Ninth Legion. The Roman governor Suetonius swore vengeance on the Britanni, and it was only because the hard-headed treasury men in Rome counselled caution, thinking of certain investments already made in the province, that the Romans did not pull out altogether.

But they stayed. Britain was also a bulwark against the northern barbarians, and a source of recruits for the Roman army: although the officers in Britain were Roman citizens, local men were recruited for the legions. No one much relished an appointment to this damp, vaguely hostile and expensive outpost. The hunting was good but after all it was only one of the 45 provinces of the Empire and as remote as Siberia for the men who had to administer it. If they had to endure it, well, then they needed some substitute for the civilised comforts of home. On the great Fosse Way leading out of the West they found hot springs as marvellous as anything in the Empire: by the end of the first century AD the Romans had built the fleshpots of Siberia, Aquae Sulis.

It is easy to compress history. The Romans came to Britain in AD 43 and quitted it in AD 410, and it is a long time ago. It sounds brief enough. But it is just short of 400 years, and if you go back 400 years from today you would be living in the reign of Queen Elizabeth I. The Romans were here a very long time. Aquae Sulis was an established Romano-British town where people became bilingual, speaking official Latin, often colloquial dog-Latin, and their own Celtic dialects. The Empire was essentially urban: the towns were important, so the area around Aquae Sulis was centred upon it. Here were markets, a great temple, probably a theatre, the headquarters of local administration both financial and military, a social centre for the large concentration of villas. Imperial estates were managed in the region, and roads ran to all parts of Britain: the Fosse, north and south west, the paved route to Londinium, to Caerleon in the west, to Vindocladia on the Dorset coast. The river, *Afon* from the Celtic, was navigable from the seaport Abonae on the Bristol Channel. Aquae Sulis was neat, and new, and built of that honey-coloured stone quarried out of the downs.

For any homesick Roman it must have been a reassuring sight on a sunny morning: the patterns of tawny tiled roofs, the glint of window glass, the high pillared and pedimented temple, and the fresco of hills beyond. And better still, the sounds and sight and warmth of the Baths.

There were several bathing establishments in Aquae Sulis, using the two main hot springs, but the chief complex was connected to the temple of Sulis-Minerva. The Romans from the

*(Opposite)* Gilded bronze head of a statue of the Roman goddess Minerva, found by a workman digging a trench near Stall Street in 1727. *(6)*

beginning had accepted the existence of the Celtic deity and added the name of their own goddess to hers. The sacred spring dedicated to this composite deity was enclosed to form a reservoir from which the waters were channelled to the various baths, and lies beneath the King's Bath we see today. People attending the Baths could toss coins, semi-precious stones, offerings of all kinds into the spring, to placate its—or their own—gods, for the spring linked secular and sacred with the Baths on one side and the temple on the other.

It is not easy now to recreate the Roman Baths from the exposed hypocausts and debris of masonry we have left, and you have to ignore the Victorian statues and balustrade against the sky above. Then, you could not see the sky, only a high vaulted roof, once timber, then of stone, where the steam rose and coiled in the shadows and sun slanted down from great clerestory windows.

Men—and women—met here not only for the sybaritic pleasure of getting clean, to be oiled, sanded, stripped with a bronze strigil blade, massaged and bathed, but for gossip, to do business and relax. It was a sort of combination of pub, rotary club, golf course and squash court. You could spend an afternoon playing vigorous ball games in the open exercise court, paved behind high walls, sit in an alcove away from the splashing of the Great Bath and buy wine and honey cakes from the endless passing traders, take a cold dip when

you felt like it, perhaps later, suitably clean, pay your respects to Sulis-Minerva.

Such people were middle class, essentially. They were cushioned by a system of which slavery was an integral part, as it was indeed for the Celts themselves. Slaves shovelled the charcoal into the pillared caverns of the hypocausts under the mosaic floors to keep the air warm, slaves massaged you, maintained the lead pipes, repaired the conduits and the paving. They were often given their freedom and some reached high office in the Roman administration—there was no lasting stigma. But without them Rome could not have functioned. And they, too, crowded the paved streets of Aquae Sulis, as did visitors from all parts of the Empire. Legionaries came on leave, for convalescence. The hot springs were a wonder of the north. Tombstones began to line the road to Londinium outside the city gates, many of them poignant, like that erected by his trade guild to 20 year old Julis Vitalis of the 20th Legion, or by her parents to little Successa Petronia, aged just three years, four months and nine days. People began to retire and settle in Aquae Sulis and the countryside around. The Julian Law, buttress of the Empire, forbade any man to carry arms: and so for 400 years Britain was more consistently at peace than ever before or since, and in dark times to follow old men remembered it as a Golden Age.

But both the Empire and the city

were being undermined, the one by an inflated economy and border invasions, the other by the sea. Throughout the third and fourth centuries AD the sea level had been rising, and with it the water table inland. The baths began to flood as culverts and drains to the river spilled water and black silt back along their courses to drown the hypocausts. Each time engineers repaired the damage, but as the effects of declining Empire began to be felt in the lack of labour, heavy taxation and growing anarchy, the impetus to keep the Baths going lessened. Central government became fragmented. People did not care to visit the town so often and urban life weakened. One day, no one came to repair the Baths of Aquae Sulis. In AD 410, when the Romano-British chiefs of Britain—for so far had it diminished from central rule—asked for help from the Emperor Honorius in Rome so that they might combat invading Scots, Picts and Saxons, he told them that the province must look after itself.

Aquae Sulis began to die. Columns cracked as the foundations shifted and subsided. Mud and earth 18 inches thick covered the pavements. A wandering Anglo-Saxon poet came upon the ruins three centuries afterward, and wrote of them:

"The roofs are fallen . . .
  Let them pour
  into a sea of stone
  the hot streams."

*(Below)* Recent excavations in the Roman reservoir below the King's Bath, with the hot spring piped off to allow work to proceed: December 1979. *(8)*

*(Above)* Soldiers of the Roman army – for whom the Baths were first built to give them a taste of home. *(7)*

*(Left)* Previous excavations in the Roman reservoir after its discovery by the city engineer in 1878. *(9)*

*(Right)* Roman central heating – one of the hypocausts. Smouldering charcoal around the pillars of tiles provided highly efficient underfloor heating. *(10A)*

*(Below Left)* Bas reliefs carved on memorial tablets in one of the sacred shrines of Aquae Sulis. *(10B)*

*(Below Right)* Roman carving of a mastiff carrying a roe deer and a hound chasing a hare – Britain was famous throughout the Empire for its hunting and breeding of hounds. *(11)*

*(Above Right)* Carved Roman altars. *(12)*

*(Right)* A theatrical mask sometimes associated with tombstones. *(13)*

*(Opposite)* Carved Gorgon's Head which once surmounted the portico of the temple of Sul-Minerva. It is Celtic in form and feeling although classical in theme. *(14)*

20

(Left) A small plunge bath in the bathing establishment. (16)

(Below) Tessellated pavement found in Bath. (17)

(Opposite) The Great Bath, once roofed with vaulted stone, colonnaded and echoing with voices. (19)

(Above) One of many lead pipes in the Roman Baths. Lead was mined by the Romans several miles south of Aquae Sulis in the Mendip Hills. (15)

(Below) One of the complex of Roman Baths. (18)

# *Hat Batha*

Out of the dark anarchy that followed the Roman abandonment of Britain came England. It took 500 years of internecine warfare between Celt and Saxon, Saxon and Norseman, Christian and pagan, king and king, before in AD 973 a 30 year old man who had already reigned for 14 years was crowned Edgar, monarch of all England, in the great Saxon abbey of St. Peter's in a small west country town called Acemanceaster, 'sick man's city'—or Hat Batha. For centuries afterwards the people of Bath celebrated the day of Edgar's coronation on that Whit Sunday, so vivid was the memory of peace brought by this descendant of King Alfred the Great. There was a glittering procession, gilded encampments on the watermeadows, feasting in the timber halls. Today, the crowning of all English kings and queens is based upon that ceremony.

Less than 100 years later, the Normans invaded. The Saxons had been both cultured, and brutal, but they did place a value on the life of a man and not upon his land: the Normans believed in land. The old freehold system was replaced by feudalism. Though slaves could no longer be bought and sold at fairs, all men now became serfs, belonging to their manorial lords who did not even speak their own language. Women were called chattels. The cattle, pigs and sheep of free men became the beef, pork and mutton of the Norman table. Saxon

landowners were dispossessed and their estates apportioned among Norman landlords. At Bath, the Benedictine priory was given by King William Rufus to one of his physicians, Bishop John de Villula, in 1088. Subsequently Bishop John, who as a doctor took a particular interest in the healing properties of the hot springs and did a lot to improve the baths, bought the whole of Hat Batha. Like many other Norman bishops he also decided to replace the Saxon abbey with a much bigger and better one—St. Peter's had by coincidence been burned down during a previous power struggle between William Rufus and a rebel Norman faction based at Bristol.

Bishop John's new church was intended to be so vast that the present Bath Abbey occupies only the site of its nave, but it was never quite finished. Nevertheless a new priory was built, and more land taken over by the monks, like that now called Prior Park, where a deep combe folds down the southern hill on the rim of the city. Dark lakes there were made to breed carp for the priory. And in its quiet cloisters may have studied the young Henry Plantagenet, who as Henry II was to temper Norman rule with his introduction of such enduring English principles as those of common law, the jury system and local government.

It was in Henry II's reign, too, that Bishop Reginald Fitzjocelin founded the Hospital of St. John in Bath, which

dates from 1180. Bishop Reginald was chosen to attend Richard I at his coronation, and in 1189 it was Richard the Lionheart who granted the city a charter giving it the right to run markets and fairs.

The city authorities began to clean the place up a bit, although the main street, Cheap Street—cheap meaning market—was then only seven feet wide with an open sewer in the middle. It must have smelt distinctly foul, especially as all kinds of rubbish were thrown into the old Bum Ditch that ran south across the watermeadows to the river, although it was actually intended to take the overflow from the hot baths.

The baths themselves were run by the monks purely for healing the sick—the Benedictine Order, if strictly followed, forbade bathing as it did eating meat. By the time the 16th century antiquarian John Leland described the baths, they had probably changed very little: there were then three, the Cross Bath, the Hot Bath, and the King's Bath. The King's was the most exclusive, the Hot was very hot, and the Cross was the largest:

"This Bath is much frequentid of people diseasid with Lepre, Pokkes, Scabbes and great Aches . . .The colour of the water is as it were a depe blew sea water, and reeketh like a seething Pot continually, having sumwhat a sulphurous and sumwhat a pleasant flavour."

*(Above)* The mediaeval baths, owned by the Benedictine monks, John Nixon 1800. *(20)*

*(Opposite)* The ponds where carp were bred for the Benedictines, now spanned by a Palladian bridge in the grounds of Prior Park, home of Ralph Allen. *(21)*

St John's Hospital. The gateway to Chapel Court, the enclave of an ancient charitable trust, established on this site since 1174. *(22)*

One of the finest Saxon churches in England at Bradford-on-Avon near Bath. *(23)*

The monks were powerful in medieval times. Almost all the land around Bath was owned either by the priory in the city, or by other religious houses as far away as Dorset. Monks, and indeed nuns, were becoming entrenched in commerce of all kinds, with their own mills, estates, rents and tithes. One trade was fast increasing: wool. English sheep were small and neat and their fleeces long and soft. Their wool was reckoned the finest quality in Europe.

The Bath priory has disappeared, but one which remains only half ruined is Hinton Priory, five miles south of the city at a village now called Hinton Charterhouse, for here was founded one of only nine Carthusian priories in England in the 13th century. You can still climb a curving stone stair to the monk's library, left silently to crumble over the centuries. On summer evenings level sun turns this place into a gold-washed shell, where you can touch the original plaster, the delicate stone vaulting of the roof. You might believe you hear the echo of those white-robed monks, although they never spoke, and as they worked at their manuscripts here the only sounds must have been the cooing of pigeons fattening in the loft beyond—and, perhaps, the sheep in the distant meadows. For although the Carthusians ate no meat, devoting their lives to solitary communion with God, the lay brothers were busily amassing fortunes for them out of wool. So

successful—possibly how undevout—was the prior of Hinton that in 1275 Henry III granted him a sheep fair of his own.

The cloth industry flourished too, and long before the industrial revolution it was bringing capitalism, trade unions, labour disputes and mechanisation to Bath. It made a lot of people rich, including Chaucer's Wife of Bath, Dame Alison, who probably lived at the important weaving village of Twerton, "bisyde Bathe." Fulling mills, which beat the woven cloth into a kind of solid serge, clacked away below massive weirs all along the Avon and its tributaries, and there are still fullers' earth works just south of Bath at Odd Down. Churchwardens' Rolls, dating from 1349, record the selling of nettles (used in dyeing), the planting of teasels used for preparing the raw wool, sheepshearing, and the building of a 'dyynge howse' at what was Bathwick ferry and is now Pulteney Bridge. The cloth industry declined rather earlier at Bath than in other areas, and no one quite knows why: it may have had something to do with pollution of the water from lead mining upriver, or even the dyeing house itself—dyeing was a dirty and smelly business—or simply with the changes in society. For in the 14th century came the Black Death.

Bath did not escape the scourge which killed half the people of England, nor the subsequent anarchy and malaise out

of which only the monasteries grew fat. None waxed plumper than those at Bath, where in 1499 the Bishop of Bath and Wells, Oliver King, found the monks dissolute and their priory church half in ruins. Nominally, the church was Bishop Oliver's Cathedral, for there he had his bishop's chair—*cathedra*—but it was quite unusable then. He appointed a new prior, William Birde, and together they planned a new abbey church which is the one we know today: only an arch in the south choir remains of the old Norman building.

Bath Abbey is late English Perpendicular in style, much restored by the great architect Sir Gilbert Scott in the 19th century, who added flying buttresses and pinnacles and meticulously worked on the fine fan vaulting of the roof. To the left of the west door you can see a stone ladder said to commemorate the dream which inspired Bishop Oliver to build his new church: he had a vision of angels going up and down a ladder with an olive tree at the foot. Prior Birde's memorial is a fine, traceried little stone chantry chapel inside the abbey.

Some 30 years later Henry VIII dissolved the monasteries and Bath Abbey was left once more neglected, until another Bishop, James Montague, revived it in the 17th century. Meanwhile Queen Elizabeth granted the city its second royal charter which gave its Corporation powers to elect a mayor

(*Opposite*) The West Front of Bath Abbey. (*24*)

(*Above Centre*) West Door of the Abbey. (*25*)

(*Above Left and Left*) Bishop Oliver King's dream in 1499 – angels ascending and descending a ladder between an olive tree and a crown, inspiring him to building the new Bath Abbey. (*26 & 26A*)

(*Above*) The East Front of the Abbey from across the River Avon and Parade Gardens. (*27*)

(*Below*) The interior of the Abbey showing the fine fan vaulting. (*28*)

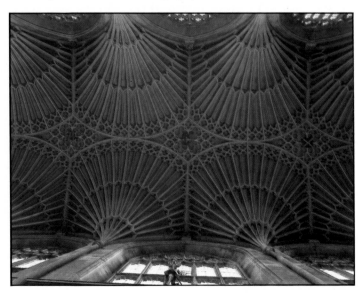

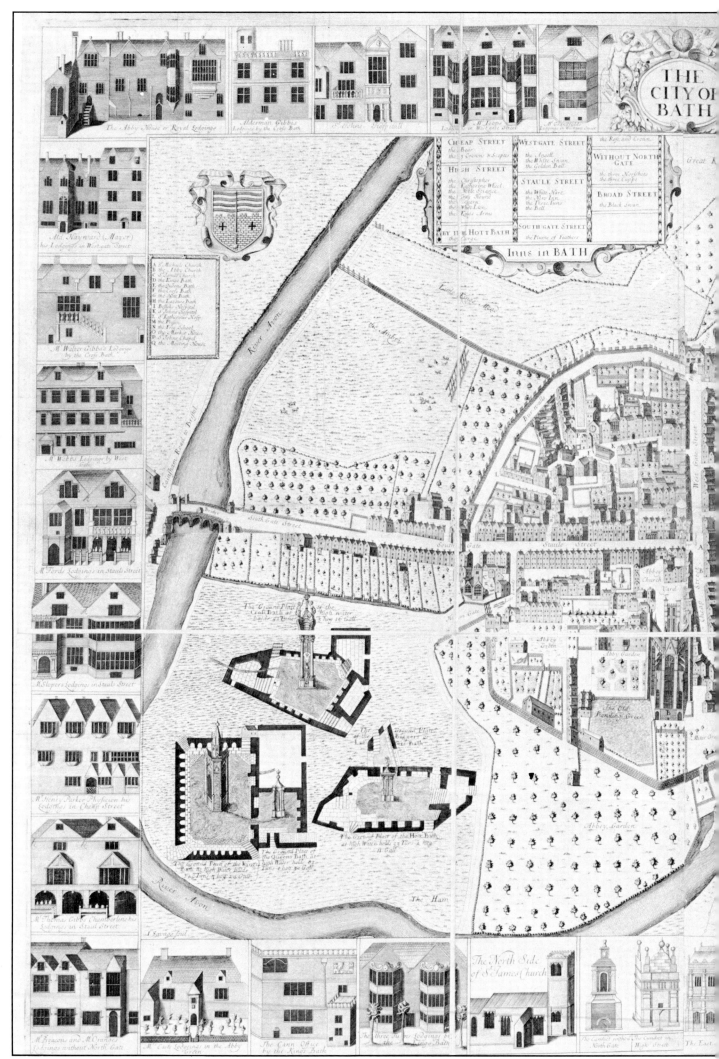

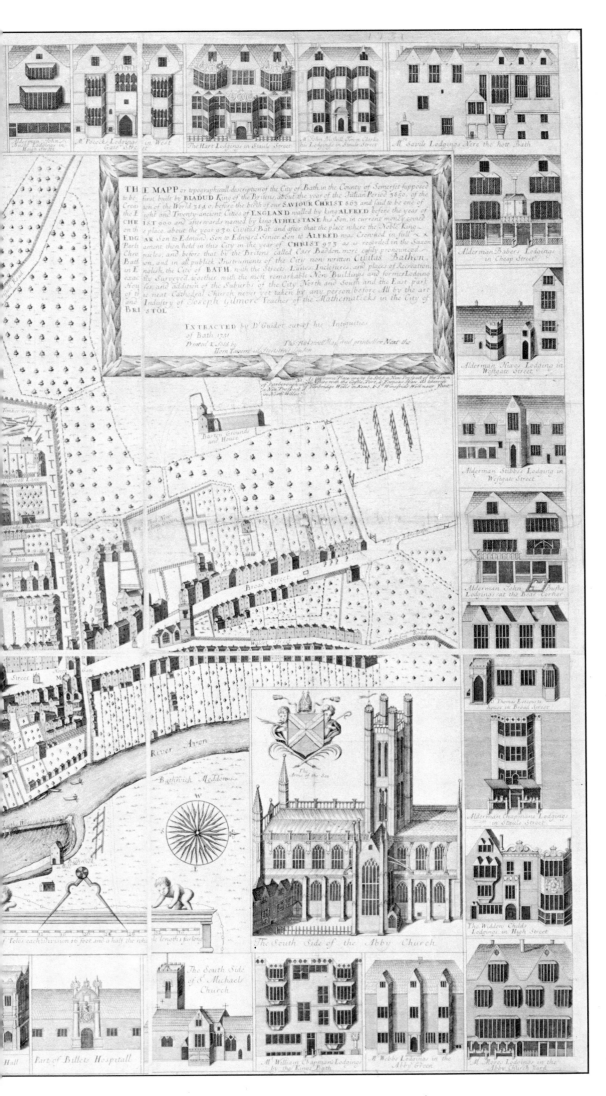

Bath as it was in 1694, just before the Georgian reconstruction, a map drawn by Joseph Gilmore of Bristol. *(29)*

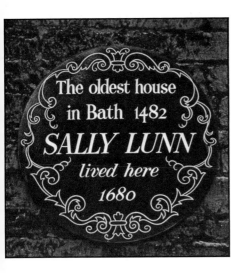

and aldermen, declaring it a "sole city of itself": the clergy, thus dismissed, owned nothing, the Corporation everything. The Abbey no longer even owned the churchyard, but at the Queen's instigation a fund was set up to repair it. Queen Elizabeth was roundly critical of the city's sewerage arrangements and her treasury minister Lord Burleigh described it as "an unsavoury town". There were considerable numbers of visitors, but only to search for cures for sickness. Not until Anne of Denmark, Queen of James I, came to find a cure for her dropsy in 1616 did the baths become rather more respectable, and the number of visitors to the city increased.

There was a lull in this progress when, a few years later, the Civil Wars broke out, to culminate in Charles I's execution in 1649. For a time the city had to raise money for the King's cause and later to bear the cost of a garrison stationed there. One battle between Royalist and Parliamentarian forces was indecisively fought on Lansdown in 1643. But on the whole neither the war nor the subsequent brief Protectorate of Cromwell much affected Bath, and people were still visiting the hot springs—not that there was much else to attract them, as a certain Dr. Jordan pointed out in 1631:

"The streets are dunghills, slaughterhouses and pig-styes. The butchers dress the meat at their own doors, while pigs wallow in the mire. The baths are bear-gardens, where both sexes bathe promiscuously."

He cannot recommend the waters for "internal use, as they could not be procured clear enough for drinking . . ."

Conscious of some shortcomings, the Corporation in 1646 issued a set of bye-laws which included the following:

" . . . No person shall presume to cast or throw any dog, bitch, or other live beast into any of the said Baths, under the penalty of three shillings and fourpence.

That no person shall thrust, cast, or throw another into any of the said Baths with his or her clothes on, under a penalty of six shillings and eightpence.

That no person or persons shall disorderly or uncivilly demean themselves in the said Baths, on pain of forfeiting five shillings."

However, things were improving, and when the Restoration had been duly celebrated with flowers and fireworks and a procession of 400 virgins through the town, Charles II's own physician recommended the health-giving qualities of Bath waters—for drinking as well as bathing.

In 1668 Samuel Pepys visited the city and although he commented that "it cannot be clean to go so many bodies together in the same water", he was agreeably surprised by the experience. Celia Fiennes, one of those indefatigable lady travellers, came to Bath in 1695 and her description of the baths is one of the most detailed. She wore a stiff canvas gown to bathe—gentlemen wore drawers and waistcoats—and the water turned everything yellow. Like all the bathers, she was carefully removed after changing into a flannel nightgown, carried to her lodgings in a sedan chair and put to bed to sweat. She said of the water: "it tastes like the water that boils eggs." Much later, Dickens' Sam Weller said it was more like warm flat irons. Both are exceedingly accurate.

At the end of the 17th century Bath was prospering on its reputation as a reasonable little country resort with very efficacious hot springs. It was attracting a lot of liverish people who could afford the fees of a multitude of quack doctors and it was getting cleaner—the Corporation even built public lavatories referred to as Houses of Ease. Its population was around 3,000. And it was all going to change.

(Opposite) Sally Lunn's House with typical pre-Georgian façade: this is thought to be the oldest house in the city. (30)

(Above) The plaque denoting the age of the house and Sally Lunn's occupancy. (31)

(Right) The mediaeval East Gate of Bath which opened out on to the river and fishmarket on the quay, showing how much the city has been raised above original ground level. (32)

# The Dream of Bath

## —and the men who made it come true

In 1694, when a Bristol mathematics teacher called Joseph Gilmore made a survey of Bath and drew a definitive map to include pictures of its "most remarkable new buildings", Bath was tiny. It was almost exactly the same size as it had been when it was Aquae Sulis, snug within what had originally been Roman boundaries. The Abbey, plainer and stubbier then without its 19th century embellishment, shouldered its way out of a close and crowded nest of half-timbered cottages, beaten earth alleyways, piggeries and gardens. The "most remarkable new buildings" were Jacobean in style, with gables and leaded windows, though they were made of stone, as Samuel Pepys noted approvingly. Bath Stone was being quarried locally, although it was little used elsewhere and thought rather inferior.

Pepys, looking out from the city walls where he walked to work off his temper over an offending sermon at the Abbey, would have seen a green and wooded landscape pieced with small fields, high hedges, deep combes and villages on the hillsides beyond the river. There was a straggle of new houses beside the dirt road leading across the watermeadows from the South Gate to the bridge at the foot of precipitous Holloway, and another out on the London Road. At the East Gate watermills turned and there was the bustle of the fishmarket on the river quay. Beyond the walls, tucked

in with orchards, were the open meadows of King's Mead, the Ambry and the Ham. In winter a miasma of coal and woodsmoke hung over the town and in summer a pervading smell of refuse and human and animal dung. It was low-lying: the East Gate, which still exists beside and below the Empire Hotel where the fishmarket used to be, shows just how low.

But England was entering a period of economic expansion and prosperity. People were beginning to have time and money for enjoying themselves—at least, the aristocracy and the rich were, and indeed there were more rich these days, including civil servants like Pepys, the upper middle classes. But in summer London was thin of company; and where else did one go? God knew the country was dull enough. Oliver Goldsmith observed:

"They wanted some place where they might have each other's company, and win each other's money, as they had done during the winter in town."

They tried Bath. It was a trifle small and tawdry, with nowhere to dance but the Town Hall, with a lot of country bumpkins—people of rank did not mix at all with the hoi polloi if they could avoid it—but the Baths were diverting, and the gaming was good, although a contemporary guidebook discreetly omits to mention that attraction.

Then, in 1702, Queen Anne went to Bath—and went again in 1703. And if it was good enough for the Queen, then it was good enough for everybody. Bath was all at once *the* place to go, and everybody who was anybody went.

"We may say now it is the resort of the sound as well as the sick and a place that helps the indolent and the gay to commit that worst of murders—to kill time";

dourly commented Daniel Defoe.

Among those summer crowds early in the 18th century was the first of the three men who were to transform Bath. He was a jaunty and essentially likeable young Welshman called Richard Nash. At 31 he had had a previously undistinguished career which included Oxford, the Guards, and the Inner Temple, from all of which he had retired with a conspicuous lack of success but with his buoyant opinion of himself quite intact. Indeed, since receiving the approval of King William III some seven years before when he organised a pageant to be presented by the Inner Temple, Nash had believed himself to have unparalleled powers of organisation.

On the other hand, he was also broke. That was the reason for his visit to Bath. It was evidently becoming a good place to make money at the gaming tables. If Nash had not done rather well that year—to the tune of

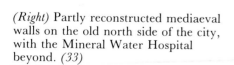

(Right) Partly reconstructed mediaeval walls on the old north side of the city, with the Mineral Water Hospital beyond. (33)

(Opposite) Richard 'Beau' Nash, Master of Ceremonies and 'King of Bath' in its heyday in the early 18th century. (34)

(*Right*) The New Assembly Rooms, or Upper Rooms, designed by John Wood the Younger and perfectly restored after destruction by bombing in 1942. *(35)*

about £1,000, so it was said, and equivalent to great wealth today—we might never have heard of him. But he did. And took over the Corporation post of Master of Ceremonies, whose main responsibility was to run the gaming rooms, when the previous incumbent died in a duel over a game of cards.

Exactly how did the son of a Carmarthen glass manufacturer come to tell the likes of the Duchess of Queensbury, the Earl of Chesterfield and indeed the Prince of Wales how to behave? Every member of the aristocracy acquiesced to his dictates as meekly as a country squire. It is a nice conundrum. Nash left very little of his own words to reveal what he was really like. Goldsmith, his friend and biographer, said:

"Nash was not born a writer; for whatever humour he might have in conversation, he used to call a pen his torpedo: whenever he grasped it, it benumbed all his faculties."

But it was an age of the quixotic, and Nash was so outrageous in his laying down of laws within his kingdom—for so Bath swiftly became—that half the fun was probably in obeying him, and laughing about it afterwards. He had a kind of innocent naïvety that made him impervious to the absurdity of his role, and once the aristocracy began to conform to his rules it became quite the thing—indeed, *de rigueur*—to do the same.

He must have had a certain charm, too. He was certainly a snob but he also had a kindly condescension, so that while beaming at a duke he was aware of some gauche youth or shy young girl who needed encouragement. He had a keen nose for humbug and disliked anyone who put on airs to which they were not entitled, and he had a wide knowledge of the finer points of etiquette and dress. Yet he himself favoured an idiosyncratic style of dress, slightly dated, and always wore a rather grubby white hat—and his favourite

food was potatoes, which he liked so much he ate them for pudding.

And Nash possessed one quality without which his regime might have been much less tolerable. He was essentially practical. The list of rules he drew up for visitors, though rather naïvely amusing, are entirely kindly and carefully thought out. He forbade duelling and the wearing of swords within the city. He persuaded the Corporation to repair main roads, to pave, clean up and light the streets. He licensed sedan chairmen and tried to control their unruly and extortionate charges. He engaged a good orchestra from London and encouraged a certain Thomas Harrison to build an Assembly Room on what is now Parade Gardens, with surrounding paved walks. Private gatherings were outlawed—which was not difficult, since accommodation was decidedly cramped and it was much easier to go out than stay in. Under Beau Nash—an ironic title—Bath

(*Right*) The first Assembly Rooms, or Lower Rooms – once on the site of Parade Gardens. *(36)*

THE LOWER ROOMS, SEEN FROM THE NORTH PARADE.

(Right) The New Assembly Rooms, or Upper Rooms, designed by John Wood the Younger and perfectly restored after destruction by bombing in 1942. (35)

about £1,000, so it was said, and equivalent to great wealth today—we might never have heard of him. But he did. And took over the Corporation post of Master of Ceremonies, whose main responsibility was to run the gaming rooms, when the previous incumbent died in a duel over a game of cards.

Exactly how did the son of a Carmarthen glass manufacturer come to tell the likes of the Duchess of Queensbury, the Earl of Chesterfield and indeed the Prince of Wales how to behave? Every member of the aristocracy acquiesced to his dictates as meekly as a country squire. It is a nice conundrum. Nash left very little of his own words to reveal what he was really like. Goldsmith, his friend and biographer, said:

"Nash was not born a writer; for whatever humour he might have in conversation, he used to call a pen his torpedo: whenever he grasped it, it benumbed all his faculties.''

But it was an age of the quixotic, and Nash was so outrageous in his laying down of laws within his kingdom—for so Bath swiftly became—that half the fun was probably in obeying him, and laughing about it afterwards. He had a kind of innocent naïvety that made him impervious to the absurdity of his role, and once the aristocracy began to conform to his rules it became quite the thing—indeed, de rigueur—to do the same.

He must have had a certain charm, too. He was certainly a snob but he also had a kindly condescension, so that while beaming at a duke he was aware of some gauche youth or shy young girl who needed encouragement. He had a keen nose for humbug and disliked anyone who put on airs to which they were not entitled, and he had a wide knowledge of the finer points of etiquette and dress. Yet he himself favoured an idiosyncratic style of dress, slightly dated, and always wore a rather grubby white hat—and his favourite

food was potatoes, which he liked so much he ate them for pudding.

And Nash possessed one quality without which his regime might have been much less tolerable. He was essentially practical. The list of rules he drew up for visitors, though rather naïvely amusing, are entirely kindly and carefully thought out. He forbade duelling and the wearing of swords within the city. He persuaded the Corporation to repair main roads, to pave, clean up and light the streets. He licensed sedan chairmen and tried to control their unruly and extortionate charges. He engaged a good orchestra from London and encouraged a certain Thomas Harrison to build an Assembly Room on what is now Parade Gardens, with surrounding paved walks. Private gatherings were outlawed—which was not difficult, since accommodation was decidedly cramped and it was much easier to go out than stay in. Under Beau Nash—an ironic title—Bath

(Right) The first Assembly Rooms, or Lower Rooms – once on the site of Parade Gardens. (36)

became rather like a large and comfortable holiday camp.

Goldsmith described the daily ritual thus established for the rest of the 18th century, and a diary of the time might have been typical of that kept by one Sophie Carey, 18 years old, eldest daughter of a widowed colonel in the Footguards who visited Bath in the 1720s with his sister Ursula, daughters Sophie and Fanny, and young son Tom.

"We arrived Tuesday: Papa in a most evil mood because we were near two days from London, leaving St. Paul's at four in the morning, with a night at the Pelican near Newbury. Crayfish very good for dinner. The guard on the coach informed me one must say 'the Bath' and not plain 'Bath'. He carried a blunderbuss as there are many highwaymen said to be on the road from Chippenham. Tom v pleased. Lodgings in Westgate Street: clean, but Aunt Ursula shocked to find notices of cock-fighting and a contest for breaking heads advertised in *The Bath Journal* in the parlour. Tom v pleased.

"They rang the Abbey bells when we reached the Bath and Papa was obliged to pay half a crown to the men. He did not expect to pay so much for everything. Two guineas for the balls, half a guinea to the bookseller. There are subscriptions to the coffee houses and the walks and the Baths. Aunt Ursula says she will bathe every morning at 8 and the sedan chairmen charge most excessively although they only carry her a short way. I have been once but agree with Papa that the water tastes unaccountably horrid, although afterwards the Pump Room is amusing and crowded with people. There are public breakfasts later in the morning, sometimes with music or lectures on Art, and hot chocolate and Sally Lunn cakes with butter which Aunt Ursula swears undoes all the good of the Baths.

"Each day at the Abbey there is a service before noon. There are some tablets on the walls to speak well of people who have died here, and Papa saw one to the memory of General Fitzjohn and said he was damned if he would pray in a place so crammed with

hypocrisy. He rides in the afternoon and visits the coffee house to talk news—there are all the newspapers here, even in the ladies' coffee houses, and booksellers circulate all new volumes published. Aunt Ursula reads or listens to the spinet before dinner, which is each day at four o'clock, and sometimes we are bidden to lectures or classes to Improve Our Minds, but Tom has been every day so far to watch the Amazing Troop Of Nine Stallions perform The Egyptian Miracle, and Fanny and I most prefer to go shopping with Mrs. Mountstewart who knows all the best shops and where to buy the best jellies.

"On Tuesdays and Thursdays the balls begin at six, v prompt, and Mr. Nash leads out the most noble lord and lady in the minuet to begin the dancing. It was my Lord Baltimore last night and I swear his coat was lined quite throughout with ermine. You cannot escape the dancing for Mr. Nash sees everyone and is quite cross if you do not get up when asked for a Country Dance. He is a kind man, I believe, but a little odd, and I swear his linen is not altogether clean. Everything must cease at 11 o'clock because he commands it. Papa says he is a fool yet harmless. Papa will not come to the balls unless Mrs. Mountstewart is there too, otherwise Tom says he spends the evening in a gaming hell."

Gambling put the savour into what Sophie's Papa would otherwise have found—as many people, like the Duchess of Marlborough, did find it—a tedious ritual. Gambling was a national passion in the early part of the 18th century. Men and women played. There was ombre, faro, basset, whist, cribbage—endless variations on the ceaseless theme of shuffling cards. Nash took his cut from the gaming rooms and certainly flourished on the proceeds. But in 1739 the Gaming Act was passed, marking the decline both in gambling and Nash's own fortunes, although he got round the total ban on faro and basset by developing alternatives like EO, Even and Odds, a form of roulette. He had an interest in another spa, Tunbridge Wells, and for a time that proved profitable too, but in 1745

another Act was passed forbidding all public gambling. By then Nash was old. Not only had his income from the gaming houses ceased, but he had long been cheated out of most of the profits.

Nash died in shabby poverty at the age of 87 in February, 1761. He was given a magnificent funeral by the Corporation and crowds turned out to pay their respects. He had never married, but his ageing mistress Juliana Papjoy left the house next to the present Theatre Royal where she had lived with him, and is said to have gone back to the country and lived alone—in a tree, some said. Nash had become an old bore, and pathetic as his kingdom changed and slipped away from him, but his achievement had been substantial. Goldsmith said of him:

". . . too much merit not to become remarkable, yet too much folly to arrive at greatness."

Three years later, the second member of this triumvirate which so altered Bath also died, but not in poverty. Ralph Allen was in contemporary terms a millionaire. Nash was actually rather better born, but he and Allen were never friends, only colleagues on certain mutual projects like the building of the Royal Mineral Water Hospital. It is evident that Allen thought Nash rather shallow and vulgar. Nash, though probably rather hurt, had his own world.

Ralph Allen was the son of a Cornish innkeeper. When he arrived in Bath in about 1710 his motive was neither financial gain nor pleasure: he was assistant to the postmistress. Even if he had wanted to, he probably had little time to join Nash's expanding empire of frivolity, since with so many visitors all busy writing and receiving letters, the post office was under severe pressure.

In 1715 Allen got wind of some sedition in the area. Hanoverian George I had succeeded Queen Anne and there was talk of Jacobite sympathisers in the west country. Allen passed the rumour to Marshal George Wade, then quartered in the city, and he made a subsequent haul of arms. Grateful to, and impressed by this serious, pleasantly mannered young man, Wade later

Bath in the early 19th century –
watercolours by R. Cruikshank.

*(37A, B, C, D, E)*

*(A)* Milsom Street and Bond Street
*(B)* Public Bathing at Bath
*(C)* Fancy Ball at the Upper Rooms
*(D)* Well known characters in the Pump
Room
*(E)* Buff Club at the Pig and Whistle

*(A)*

*(B)*

*(C)*

*(D)*

*(E)*

*(Opposite)* Ralph Allen, one of the three
great Georgian builders of Bath. This
portrait now hangs in the Royal
National Hospital for Rheumatic
Diseases of which he was a
benefactor. *(42)*

(*Left*) Beau Nash's front door. *(43)*

(*Below*) Marshal Wade's town house in the Abbey Church Yard: Ralph Allen was his protégé and son-in-law. *(44)*

*(Below)* Rare 18th century watercolour by Thomas Bampfylde showing Ralph Allen's house and his stone wharfs on the river at Widcombe. *(45)*

encouraged a match between Allen and his natural daughter. Allen was lucky in his father in law. Wade, who later built the great military roads in the Highlands of Scotland and became Member of Parliament for Bath, was a generous man. It was with his backing that Allen developed the main postal routes across country and earned £6,000 from the Post Office, and later became involved with various commercial projects. In 1724 Ralph Allen put money into the new Avon Navigation company which was to make the river navigable to Bristol. Two years later, aware of the value of this export route, he bought and began to develop the

stone quarries on Combe Down.

By 1726 there had been little physical expansion of the city despite new buildings within it, like the Assembly Rooms, the rebuilt Pump Room, façades in Broad Street and Green Street. Certainly a new style was apparent, a cooler classicism. Inigo Jones's precept that buildings should be "solid, proportionable, according to the rules, masculine and unaffected", was influential, as was Christopher Wren's new work in London. The old rococo forms and details were out of date. And the local Bath Stone, though disdained by London architects, was admirably suited to this new fashion. Anyway,

Ralph Allen reckoned, it had really not been shown off sufficiently. He was a shrewd businessman. Not only did he discern the intrinsic quality of the Combe Down stone, but he knew that Bath was on the verge of widescale development and that any stone at all was going to be in demand. And now, with the river navigable, it could be exported as well.

You can see the neat houses of Allen's quarry workers at Combe Down today, and the uneven surface of Firs Field hides the old workings—stone mines, they called them. In the deep combe dropping down to the city, where Bishop John de Villula bred his lakes of

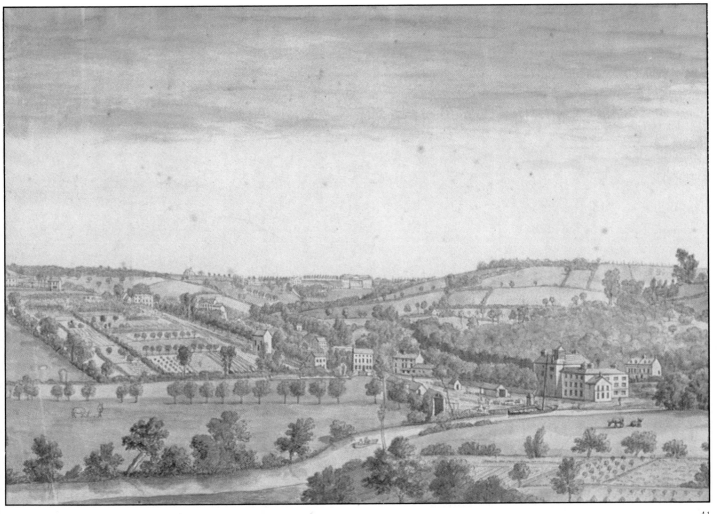

(Above) Palladian Bridge and Prior Park, designed by John Wood the Elder for Ralph Allen. (46)

(Left) Prior Park. (47)

(Below) Bust of David Garrick, famous 18th century actor, over the pub doorway next to the Theatre Royal. (48)

carp, Allen built a vast mansion called Prior Park. This, he let it mutely declare to critical London architects, is what Bath Stone can do.

Down what is now called Ralph Allen's Drive he built a railway to carry the blocks of stone, some of them weighing six tons, down to the river wharf at Widcombe. The railway was one of the wonders of the day—and it enabled Allen to cut his prices for stone from 10s. to 7s. 6d. a ton.

He was a curious mixture, this quiet man of whom the cultured and generous Squire Allworthy of Henry Fielding's novel *Tom Jones* is a portrait. He liked the company of writers like Fielding, and regular visitors at Prior Park included the poet Alexander Pope, actors David Garrick and James Quin, William Pitt and the painter Gainsborough. Allen had a gift for hospitality and yet a certain Philip Thicknesse, notorious for a sharp tongue, suggested that his humility was somewhat assumed and that he was in fact a man "deeply charged with pride." Certainly he did not like Pope referring to him in a poem as "low born", and made him change it to "humble."

Yet without Ralph Allen, and especially his business acumen, it is doubtful whether a young architect called John Wood would ever have come to Bath. No one knows whether it was Allen who first suggested that Wood

should exercise his talent there, but it is possible, and certainly he encouraged this quick-tempered, single-minded young man from Yorkshire to believe that he could fulfil his dream of building a Palladian city here in Bath.

Andrea Palladio was a 16th century Italian architect who returned to Roman architecture to find inspiration for rules of proportion and balance which he developed exquisitely in his own designs, especially for country villas around the Veneto. In 1663, his book of his research and drawings was published in England. John Wood was one of his disciples. But Wood was also, in his own right, greatly gifted.

He first worked for Lord Bingley in Yorkshire as a surveyor and architect, and this peer brought him to London, where he was subsequently employed by the Duke of Chandos both in the capital and on his property in Bath. No doubt Wood then recognised his opportunity. Ralph Allen's Avon Navigation scheme was well ahead. Wood wrote:

"When I found Work was likely to go on, I began to turn my thoughts towards the improvement of the city by building; and for this purpose I procured a plan of the town, which sent me into Yorkshire, in the summer of the year 1725, where I, at my leisure hours, formed one design for the ground at the north west corner of the city; and another for the land on the north east

side of the town and river. After my return to London, I imparted my first design to Mr. Gay, an eminent surgeon in Hatton Garden, and proprietor of the land . . .''

His designs included a Royal Forum, a Grand Circus and an Imperial Gymnasium—"from a work of that kind taking its rise at first in Bath during the time of the Roman emperors.''

Mr. Gay, keen at first, became less so later, and the Corporation was not at all co-operative when the impatient Mr. Wood presented them with a scheme for completely rebuilding the city. But John Wood persevered. He was enchanted by Bath. He wrote a long essay about it. In 1727 he settled in the city and in the same year his son, also called John, was born. Not that Wood set out to be popular. He dismissed the work of other local architects like Thomas Greenway, who built St. John's court and probably did some rebuilding in Broad Street and elsewhere, and called him a stonecutter. He developed a positive hatred of John Strahan, who developed the area around Kingsmead including Kingsmead and Beauford Squares, and whose style was decidedly more baroque than Palladian—Rosewell House in Kingsmead Square is probably his design. And Strahan was to supplant Wood as architect for the Avon Navigation company, which did not help.

*(Above Left)* Kingsmead Square, laid out by John Wood's contemporary and rival John Strahan. *(49)*

*(Above Right)* Ralph Allen's town house, designed by John Wood the Elder and tucked behind York Street today – once it had an open view on gardens. *(50)*

*(Right)* Sham Castle, the folly built for Ralph Allen, with a view across to Camden Crescent. *(51)*

Nevertheless, Wood finally made a start. He first worked on Ralph Allen's town house, now tucked down an alley off York Street: this house was once open to the view of Claverton and Bathampton Downs, and you can see high on the far hill the little folly of Sham Castle, built to enhance the scene and designed for Allen by Richard Jones, a later rival of Wood's. A new assembly room, and St. John's Hospital, were also among Wood's projects at this time: but for him the important achievement was that he persuaded the cautious Mr. Gay to lease the land to the north west of the city on which he planned to begin his Great Design. It was the site of Queen Square.

To finance the project, Wood first designed the elevations of the square and then sub-leased the sites for individual houses to builders, giving them complete freedom to plan the interiors to suit their prospective tenants, but demanding strict adherence to his exterior design. So many people wanted to secure rented accommodation for the Bath season that the builders had no problems in getting long tenancies, which their bankers then accepted as security against advances of cash.

Queen Square was completed in seven years. It has been marked by the war, slightly altered, and is not yet all cleaned, but it should be seen as the forecourt of a palace, the north front dominating the square. That north side is in fact seven large houses forming a perfect single composition of columns, Corinthian capitals, cornice and pediment. Great trees obscure Queen Square today although Wood planned a formal garden of parterre beds planted with shrubs and neatly enclosed by espaliered limes and low balustrade wall. He also designed the obelisk in the centre, raised as a tribute to the Prince of Wales by Beau Nash, who persuaded an unwilling Alexander Pope to write its inscription.

*(Right)* Queen Square. *(52)*

*(Above Left)* North Parade. *(53)*

*(Above Right)* South Parade. *(54)*

*(Right)* Gay Street. *(55)*

*(Top)* Palladian frieze in John Wood's Circus. *(56)*

*(Above Left)* The Circus, towards Gay Street. *(57)*

*(Above Right)* One of the 33 houses in The Circus, showing the Roman Doric, Ionic and Corinthian columns. *(58)*

*(Right)* The Circus, from the south. *(59)*

Wood next turned to what he called his Royal Forum. He built the Parades, plain, sunlit terraces of pale amber stone against the backdrop of Bathwick's high green hill, broad paved walks lifted on vaults above the marshy riverbank, and Pierrepont Street behind. But it was only in the last year of his life, 1754, that he began the only great work that fully realises his vision. When he died at the age of 50 on the 23rd of May, he had seen the beginning of his Grand Circus.

His son, John Wood the Younger, had been working with his father, and now continued to complete this last creation. The Circus is a Roman amphitheatre translated into domestic architecture. It is composed of three segments of 33 houses in all, each varying in size and all built of three storeys richly chiselled with Roman Doric, Ionic and Corinthian plain-shafted three-quarter columns. There are friezes, garlands, masks, parapets and great stone acorns. When it was built the Circus curved round an open space of paving and cobbles with a well in the centre to serve the houses, and the great trees of today, though beautiful in themselves, are alien to what is so essentially an urban design.

John Wood the Younger was not just a dutiful son. He too was an architect of vision, and perhaps less acknówledged than he should be. It was he who built Brock Street, linking the Circus with what is the summit of Palladian perfection in Bath, the Royal Crescent.

Within eight years of the laying of the foundation stone in 1767, the 30 houses of this exquisite semi-ellipse overlooking a green lawn were curled serenely in the sun. Royal Crescent is designed with the utmost economy and simplicity and yet its proportions, its balance and grace, combine delicacy of detail to make you catch your breath. However long you live in Bath, this Crescent can still rest the eyes and spirit.

In 1771 Wood the Younger completed the Assembly Rooms—the Upper Rooms, as they were called in contrast to those near the Parades. Ten years later he died, aged only 54. Little fuss was made at his death. There were by then plenty of other architects and builders vying for acclaim.

*(Overleaf, verso)* Brock Street, built by John Wood the Younger to link his father's Circus with his own Royal Crescent. *(60 & 61)*

*(Overleaf)* Aerial view – the triumph of John Wood, father and son. *(62)*

*(Opposite)* The glory of the Royal Crescent. *(63)*

*(Below Left)* Interior of the Assembly Rooms. *(64)*

*(Below Right)* Robert Adam's Pulteney Bridge. *(65)*

There was Robert Adam, who in 1770 built that lovely fragile span of Pulteney Bridge for William Pulteney, and who might have gone on to build Bathwick New Town had not that less than scrupulous city architect Thomas Baldwin taken over the project. Baldwin was the designer of the Guildhall. He produced the grand symmetry of Great Pulteney Street, 1,100 feet long and 100 feet wide, along with Laura Place, the new Pump Room, and a good deal of other new building in the city. It is possible that he also designed the charming Widcombe Crescent, and he worked on many houses around the city. The Holburne of Menstrie Museum, once the Sydney Hotel set in Sydney Gardens—the Vauxhall Gardens of Bath, glittering with lights, fireworks and music—was built by the architect Charles Harcourt Masters, but probably from Baldwin's original designs for it. But Thomas Baldwin rather overdid his private speculation. He had a partner, John Eveleigh, who made patent water

closets as well as designing Grosvenor
on the A4, Somerset Place, and
Camden Crescent, that airy scoop of
morning sun off Lansdown; both went
bankrupt in 1793, and Baldwin was
sacked from his Corporation post.

Their fierce rival was John Palmer,
who succeeded Baldwin as city architect,
and put the final touches to the Pump
Room. He designed Lansdown
Crescent, lovely in itself but revealing
the more plainly classical style which
followed Wood's pure Palladianism.
Later, John Pinch added Cavendish
Crescent, Cavendish Place and Sion
Hill Place among other early 19th
century delights, graceful and elegant.
There followed, too, a lot of
ecclesiastical building, like the neo-
Gothic St. Mary's Bathwick, and the
Friends Meeting House in York Street
which is rather incongruously of the
Greek Revival style. They marked not
only the fundamental changes in
architecture of the city, but in its life
and character.

Subtly, after the death of Nash, Bath ceased to be so exclusive a haunt of the *beau monde.* As more lodging houses were built, so more people could rent one for the season; as they became more comfortable and spacious, it was easier to entertain privately. The end of public gaming gave way to private card parties. The balls became rather less formal. In 1771 Tobias Smollett wrote *Humphrey Clinker* and put a decidedly jaundiced view into the letters of his character Matthew Bramble:

"Every upstart of fortune, harnessed in the trappings of the *mode,* presents himself at Bath . . . men of low birth, and no breeding, have found themselves suddenly translated into a state of affluence unknown to former ages. Such is the composition of what is called the fashionable company at Bath; where a very inconsiderable proportion of genteel people are lost in a mob of impudent plebeians . . ."

Christopher Anstey, scholar and parson, also took a less than adulatory tone when he published the scurrilously clever *New Bath Guide* in 1766, a long poem in the form of letters written home by a family visiting Bath for the first time—Simkin Blunderhead, sister Prudence, cousin Jenny and maid Tabitha Runt, to be precise. It is nevertheless affectionate, witty and great fun, with characters like Mrs. Danglecub and Lady Bumfidget, and if the picture it paints reveals just how unexclusive Bath had become, it is at the same time a delightfully accurate portrait. As Simkin writes to his Mother at the outset of their visit, when they received the requisite attendance of a doctor:

"He determin'd our Cases at length (God preserve us).
I'm Bilious, I find, and the Women are Nervous;
Their Systems relax'd, and all turned topsy turvy,
With Hypochondriacs, Obstructions, and Scurvy . . ."

*(Above)* Inside the Guildhall. *(66)*

*(Right)* Great Pulteney Street. *(67)*

(*Top*) Glimpse of the Pump Room, from the Abbey Churchyard. (*68*)

(*Above Left*) Bath Water fountain in The Pump Room – ''Shall we try the waters?'' (*69*)

(*Above*) The Man Who Asked for a Glass of Whisky in Bath Pump Room – cartoon H. M. Bateman. (*71*)

(*Right*) An original Bath chair (*70*)

*(Top)* Camden Crescent. *(72)*

*(Above Right)* Placard announcing a performance of The Messiah at Mr Herschel's Benefit-Concert, 15th April 1778. *(74)*

*(Left)* The Holburne of Menstrie Museum. *(73)*

But Smollett also lets Lydia Melford give her view of Bath in *Humphrey Clinker*—a little less cynically. She innocently delights in this "new world"; she finds (at first) everything "gaiety, good humour and diversion". Wood's Circus and Parades are like sumptuous palaces, and all the other new buildings look to Lydia like enchanted castles raised on hanging terraces.

There was certainly a mix of societies, and an increasingly sleazy side to the city. Prostitutes accommodated all kinds of clients down in Avon Street, by the river—the red light district for long afterwards. But there was, too, a lighter and more civilised society, of which

Richard Sheridan wrote so deftly in *The Rivals,* first produced in 1775 and set, like his later *School for Scandal,* in Bath. His Lydia Languish was no doubt based upon the beautiful Elizabeth Linley, who came of a noted musical family and eloped with Sheridan to escape an unwelcome marriage.

And although the fashionable *ton* was now turning to Brighton and other seaside resorts for its pleasures, Bath was attracting many people in the arts and letters. Dr. Johnson came to visit his Mrs. Thrale in Bath, until she married a Mr. Piozzi; already by the end of the century Jane Austen was visiting friends in the Paragon, and a

young German called William Herschel was playing the organ in the Octagon chapel while thinking about the telescope he was in the middle of making—he discovered the planet Uranus in 1781. In the season, extended now to spring, the local *Bath Journal* and *Bath Register* were both full of lists of those arriving in Bath. It was not so frothy as it had been, not so public or so ostentatious, but people had begun to like living there, not just staying for a month or two, and it was acquiring a flavour of its own—a drier, stiller wine than champagne.

In the local *Bath Register and Western Advertiser* is news of the French wars, a

*(Above)* Lansdown Crescent. *(75)*

*(A)*

*(B)*

*(C)*

*(Top)* Comforts of Bath
– by T. Rowlandson. *(76A, B, C)*

*(Above Right)* Trim Street and Trim
Bridge. *(79)*

*(Above)* Bathwick at night. *(80)*

*(Right)* Abbey Green at night. *(81)*

*(Right)* Local, National and International news in the 18th century – the *Bath Chronicle* of Thursday 22nd February 1776. *(82)*

*(Below)* Behind the facades. *(83)*

plan to build another canal, notices of schools opening for the forthcoming term and advertisements for apprentices. A handsome bay saddle gelding is for sale at 25 guineas. You can buy Curious Cowslip Tea at 12s. a pound, or ladies' French stays at £1. 5s. 0d. A certain Mary Severne, an Infant just turned Sixteen, has run off with her father's groom: said Mary Severne is tall and lusty for her age, with freckles and red hair—the Clergy are Cautioned not to publish the banns of marriage for these two persons. . . . A pleasantly situated house in a genteel neighbourhood is up for auction and Dr. Wheatley recommends his

Remedies for the Itch. One James May has been sentenced at Assize to be transported for seven years for stealing a cloth coat and a pair of corduroy breeches.

It is 1794. A century since Joseph Gilmore drew his map of the city. In that time the population has grown from around 3,000 to over 30,000. The old narrow alleys, the dark gabled houses, have almost completely been obliterated—virtually none of Gilmore's "most remarkable new building" is left. You could say that Bath has been desecrated by speculative builders, developers who saw a chance to make money: that much of the Georgian

building is not even very competent, the backs of exquisite crescents hardly matching their elegant fronts. Under the new streets are stone vaults to raise the whole city high above the debris of the old. It stretches far beyond the ancient walls, to the village of Bathwick, to the slopes of Lansdown, the fields beyond Royal Crescent. It is probably the most beautiful little city in Europe.

# The People of Bath

What makes any city in the world? Its people. And the people of Bath, of yesterday and today, still leave their imprint upon the city. It seems a good idea to meet a few.

Adelard of Bath

Such a monk as this, a black-clad Benedictine, was the scholar Adelard of the 12th century, who travelled widely in Europe and the Middle East and translated Euclid and Ptolemy from Arabic. For a time he stayed in England to write a great work on astronomy, and dedicated it to the young Henry Plantagenet whom he probably taught in the cloisters of the priory at Bath. Perhaps it was from Adelard that Henry II learned some of his clear and scholarly wisdom. *(84)*

Christopher Anstey

Poets were forever writing about the delights of Bath in the late 18th century but none so cleverly or satirically as Christopher Anstey, a fellow of King's College, Cambridge, and a parson. His *New Bath Guide* caused a great stir when it appeared in 1766, describing the visit of a family called the Blunderheads to Bath, and including such characters as Mrs. Danglecub, Lady Pandora MacScurvey, General Sulphur and Lady Bumfidget as well as quite delicious pictures like that of the King's Bath:

" 'Twas a glorious sight to behold the fair sex

All wading with gentlemen up to their necks,

And view them so prettily tumble and sprawl

In a great smoking kettle as big as our hall;

And today many persons of rank and condition

Were boil'd by command of an able physician.''

This double silhouette of Anstey and his wife Anne was made by Jacob Spornberg, who invented profiles painted ''in the Etruscan manner'', with a vermilion red base enamel against a black background beneath convex glass. Advertising his studio in Lilliput Alley in 1790, he offered his services to the nobility: ''2 sittings of 3 minutes each.'' *(85)*

## Emma Hart (Left)

She must have been bewitching even as a young servant girl when she worked for the Linley family in Orchard Street in the late 1770s. A descendant of the family still recalls how "very naughty" Emma was. Since Horatio Nelson, as a young post-captain, convalesced for a time just across the road in Pierrepont Street, perhaps he gave that very naughty maid a second glance. . . . Later, she became Lady Hamilton. (86, 87)

*By permission of the National Portrait Gallery.*

## Arthur King (Right)

"My father was a Bath solicitor and I followed him into the profession. I was born in the city. As a small boy I can remember when they put turf down in Darlington Street to deaden the sound of the carriages and cars, because someone was ill in one of the houses. I used to go to church at St. Mary's Bathwick, with Nanny, but she was obliged to go up to the gallery: the Quality sat in the centre aisle, Trade and Professional people in the side aisles, and Servants in the gallery, you see. That was in the 1920s. In those days you could buy a Georgian house for a song, about £100 in the late 1920s and 30s. Many stood empty. Small private hotels were full of geriatric gentry trying to keep up the old caste system. The first developers moved in then. After the last war, a great many little Georgian artisans' terraced houses were pulled down because they were considered unfit for human habitation, although today they would be lovingly restored. There are a great many flats in Bath today, although until comparatively recently internal bathrooms were not permitted, and that's why if you look at the backs of some of these Georgian houses, you can see bathrooms stuck on the outside, like warts." (88)

William Friese Greene *(Left)*

At the turn of this century, William Friese Greene was a young and ambitious photographer with a business in The Corridor in Bath. In his spare time he worked on perfecting his great invention: the cinematograph, which led the way to modern cinema today. But he was never really acknowledged in his lifetime, and when the first silent films were making fortunes for everyone else, he died impoverished in 1921. This portrait is from one of his business cards. *(90)*

Guinea Pig Jack *(Right)*

Old soldiers like Guinea Pig Jack were often seen in Bath after the Great War. He kept his guinea pigs in a basket, and trained them to fall down dead at command—then jump smartly up again when told the Law was on its way. *(91)*

(Above) Wiliam Hoare's painting of Dr. Oliver and Mr. Pierce, (Physician and Surgeon), examining patients at the Royal Mineral Water Hospital in 1742. (89A)

*Reproduced by permission of the Royal National Hospital for Rheumatic Diseases.*

John Blinkhorn (Right)
''I've been baking Bath Buns for about ten years now. I suppose I do about 3,000 a week, more in the summer. They're made of eggs, flour and yeast: you make a sponge dough with egg and yeast and a little flour and leave it to ferment and rise, then shape the soft dough by hand and add the hard lumps of sugar—if a Bath Bun hasn't got a lump of sugar baked in it, then it's not a Bath Bun. They have to be very very light. If they don't taste right, out they go and we start again. You brush the top with a bit of egg, nib sugar and currants.'' The recipe for Bath Buns is very old: Jane Austen was ''disordering'' her stomach with Bath Buns in 1801, they were so delicious. The Noted Old Red House was founded in 1798 in New Bond Street and today still flourishes. They still have a recipe for the original Bath Oliver biscuits, too, said to have been invented by Dr. William Oliver as an alternative to Bath Buns for his liverish patients. (89)

Chris Flannery (*Left*)

"I'm a Sister here at the Royal National Hospital for Rheumatic Diseases, which used to be the Royal Mineral Water Hospital built by John Wood. I'm a State Registered Nurse working for my Diploma of Nursing. I was born in Bath—my father is in the Ministry of Defence here—and I've worked here at the hospital for two years. We have about 100 patients, mostly suffering from rheumatoid arthritis and diseases of the spine. The average age is about 50—a lot of young people get arthritis which one doesn't always realise. We do a lot of research here, and we are one of the few hospitals specialising in rheumatic diseases. Hot water is part of the treatment and we have a pipeline to the hospital from the hot springs." (*92*)

Richard Brinsley Sheridan (*Right*)

Sheridan had his Irish father's charm and his literary mother's talent with words, and his first play, *The Rivals,* has in it echoes of the Great Bath Scandal which he caused when he eloped with the beautiful Elizabeth Linley, whisking her off in a post-chaise to Calais to save her from the clutches of the dissipated Major Matthews. On his return he fought a duel with the wicked Major Matthews, was heroically wounded, and just managed to survive with the devoted nursing of his bride whom he finally married publicly and properly in London. (*93*)

*By permission of the National Portrait Gallery.*

## King Edgar *(Above)*

Edgar was only 30 when he was crowned at Bath in AD 973, and only 16 when he first reigned. He was the first King of All England, and his brief time of peace was long remembered. Ever since that joyous Whit Sunday, Edgar's coronation has set the precedent for the ceremony used at crowning the kings and queens of England. *(98)*

## Rashleigh Francis Ellsworth *(Right)*

"I'm one of two Senior Traffic Wardens. There's 20 of us altogether in Bath, though sometimes you might think they're everywhere. . . . I was born and bred here, been in the building trade most of my life until I became a traffic warden 13 years ago. I wouldn't want to live anywhere else. And I don't mind being a traffic warden. On the whole people are reasonable. We've only had to prosecute about three for assault in the past few years. You have to be calm. You can't lose your temper or you'd never find it. Lots of people think we have to issue a certain number of tickets, but that's poppycock. I'd rather see a clear street than somebody slapping tickets on. I'm a motorist myself, after all." *(99)*

## William Smith *(Right)*

The young William Smith came to work on the Somerset Coal Canal which linked the Somerset coalfields to the south west of Bath with the Kennet and Avon canal at Limpley Stoke, and it was then that he became interested in the local rock formation. In 1799, when he was living in the small hamlet of Midford on the old Somerset Coal Canal, he drew a map of a five mile area around Bath and meticulously coloured in the geological features. It is the first geological map known, and it is still accurate today. In 1815 he published his great geological map of England, the first ever made. He was one of the founders of the modern science and not only an expert on fossils and rocks but a superb engineer—he was once called in when the hot springs at Bath stopped flowing and with typical competence restored the water to its proper course. But his passion for geology never made him any money. He had to sell his fossil collection to the British Museum. He died in 1839 on his way to a meeting of the British Association. *(96)*

*Reproduced by permission of the Geological Society of London.*

## Tobias Smollett *(Left)*

Smollett was a doctor, which was probably why he took a rather less rose-coloured view of Bath than writers less aware of its unpleasant side. If you want to know the corrupt and vicious underworld of what was superficially so frivolous a city, read Smollett's *Roderick Random, Peregrine Pickle* and *Humphrey Clinker,* all published in the late 18th century. He was merciless in his descriptions:

"Even the wives and daughters of low tradesmen, who, like shovel-nosed sharks, prey upon the blubber of those uncouth whales of fortune, are infected with the same rage of displaying their importance. . . . There is always a great show of the clergy at Bath; none of your thin, puny, yellow, hectic figures, exhausted with abstinence and hard study—but great overgrown dignitaries and rectors, with rubicund noses and gouty ankles, or broad bloated faces, dragging along great swag bellies; the emblems of sloth and indigestion." *(101)*

**Ernest Bowler** *(Left)*

Mr. Bowler is 90. His grandfather, J. B. Bowler, founded the family business of Bowler's in 1872 and it became well known in Bath as a general engineering works, brass foundry, mineral water factory and a shop which sold everything from a particular brass nut to a Victorian decorated lavatory. "My grandfather never threw anything away. None of us did. I was apprenticed as an engineer myself, and went into the family firm in about 1910—all of us worked there, the girls as well, and we had a lot of fun because there were a lot of us. It was because my grandfather never threw anything away that they've made this museum here; when the corporation decided to pull down the old shop, Russell Freer bought the whole stock. Now they've put it all back together, the shop, my grandfather's office, the foundry and the mineral water factory, all as it was. I didn't like seeing it. It made me sad, so many years of old memories in it." The Camden Works Museum, housing the Bowler Collection, is at Morford Street north of the Assembly Rooms. *(94)*

**William Hoare** *(Right)*

Bath was full of portrait painters. Amongst the most successful was William Hoare, who married a Bath girl in 1739. He painted everyone who was anyone in the city, and although not a great artist he was painstaking, competent and scholarly. He was also an urbane, civilised man and people liked to visit his studio to be seen there. He also encouraged young artists like Thomas Lawrence, with the generosity of a man aware of his own limitations. He was one of the first members of the Royal Academy. *(109)*

Anna Ledbury *(Right)*

I'm ten. I am in the third form at Bath High School, and every morning I walk down the hill from where we live on Lansdown to school in Lansdown Crescent. My favourite subjects are crafts and music—I can play the violin, the recorder and the piano. I would *actually* prefer to live in the country, because although we have a cat I'd like more animals; except that actually I don't like cows; but if I can't live in the country, then I'd rather live in Bath than anywhere else. I always show people round the Roman Baths when they come to stay with us, and I like doing that. Sometimes I've thought I could see somebody swimming in the water. It makes me feel creepy. I think one of the Romans must have stayed behind.'' *(97)*

Samuel Pepys *(Right)*

''Up at four o'clock, being by appointment called up to the Cross Bath, where we were carried one after another, myself, and wife, and Betty Turner, Willet and W. Hewer. And by and by, although we designed to have done before company come, much company come; very fine ladies; and the manner pretty enough, only methinks it cannot be clean to go so many bodies together in the same water. . . . Carried away, wrapped in a sheet, and in a chair, home; and there one after another thus carried, I staying above two hours in the water, home to bed, sweating for an hour . . .'' *(100)*

*By permission of The National Portrait Gallery.*

Brian Branson (*Left*)
"There are several fishmongers in Bath: it's a good city for wet fish, although it's so far inland. We buy most of our fish from Cornwall, when it comes into Bristol fishmarket at about five a.m. We probably sell about 100 stone of fish a week. People in Bath appreciate some of the more unusual fish, like red mullet, sea bass and squid—we get a lot of Chinese buying squid, about 10 stone a week. Messy to clean, all the black ink, but good. We sell John Dory, too. That's the fillet steak of fish, though the look of it puts people off a bit. Me, I like sprats. People think they're small herrings but they're not; a sprat is a sprat. Don't take the heads off or gut them, just shake them in seasoned flour and quickly fry 'em in fat—delicious. And cheap." (106)

Captain Francis Holburne (*Right*)

Francis Holburne was a captain in the 3rd Regiment of Footguards during the Peninsular Wars under the Duke of Wellington. On the 23rd of April, 1814, he died at Bayonne. A musket ball had entered his left foot and had become infected: he died of tetanus. Ironically, peace was signed on the following day. It was his brother Thomas Holburne who later gathered the great collection of paintings, porcelain, glass and other beautiful things which is now housed at the Holburne of Menstrie Museum: Thomas himself was a young midshipman at Trafalgar. In a glass case at the Holburne of Menstrie Museum you can see the letter sent by Francis's father to his sister Mrs. Cussons, informing her of his son's death. The letter, written in a strong hand, is marked with tears. (105)

## Priscus (Left)

Priscus, the son of Toutius, was a stonemason from Chartres, and one of many visitors to Aquae Sulis from all parts of the Roman Empire who raised such small private altars as this before they left. Priscus has inscribed this stone with a message of thanks to Sulis, goddess of the springs. Perhaps he recovered from an illness during his stay, or was visiting the stone quarries at Combe Down and asked the local deity's help in negotiating some business deal. Like the tombstones found outside the city gates, such inscriptions reveal something of the people of Aquae Sulis. Even the poorest had family shrines and household gods to help with daily problems, and people put up inscriptions to various gods for all sorts of reasons—to thank them for a safe journey, for recovery, or even a good day's hunting. *(102)*

## William Herschel (Right)

A young and impoverished Hanoverian, William Herschel arrived in Bath in 1772 after deserting from his German regiment, then under English command against the French, some years before. He was a polished musician and became conductor of the Assembly Rooms orchestra, subsequently playing the organ at the Octagon and becoming much in demand for concerts. He also taught music, and one of his pupils, a certain Mr. Bernard, was quite startled by Mr. Herschel's lodgings:

". . . they resembled an astronomer's much more than a musician's, being heaped up with globes, maps, telescopes, reflectors etc., under which his piano was hid, and the violincello, like a discarded favourite, skulked away in one corner."

Actually Herschel—and his brother Alexander—were ambitious musicians. But astronomy did perhaps come first for William. On 13th March, 1781, he discovered the planet Uranus. *(107)*

*By permission of the National Portrait Gallery.*

Philip Littlewood *(Left)*

"I decided I wanted to be a verger when I was 16; I'm 20 now. There are two vergers here at the Abbey. We work very long hours—I've never worked less than 45 hours in a week, looking after things and getting ready for services and concerts. I like Bath Abbey because it's small and compact, you can feel part of it: it's really a big parish church. I like its simplicity. It's Low Church. And I like the memorial tablets on the walls, although some people don't. Someone once wrote:

'These walls adorned with monument
    and bust
  Show how Bath Waters serve to lay
    the dust.'

The inscriptions do rather flaunt the social virtues of people who probably weren't always very good at all, but they are fascinating to read. They speak of people. And another thing I like very much is Prior Birde's chantry—that's beautiful." *(104)*

Albert William Frost *(Right)*

"I've been 40 years in this shop in Walcot. The cattle market's just round the corner and when I came here, there were sheep pens out in the road, and 20 pubs in Walcot then. Opposite me is the old cattle trough they built. My grandfather had a timber yard in Beauford Square, and myself, I'm a woodcarver by trade. I was in the Royal Flying Corps in the Great War when I was 21—four years in France. I'm 83 now and except for the arthritis in my hands I'm keeping fit—that's because I sleep alone, you know. I was married for 39 years but not any more. I look after meself. Mind you, I'm looking for a rich widow. Not a rich spinster—she wouldn't have the experience, wouldn't know the ropes, would she? Hey, don't you listen to my nonsense. I do all right, selling reproduction furniture. Don' you worry about me." *(103)*

The Linley Sisters

Elizabeth and Maria Linley were both beautiful and accomplished singers of a gifted family in Bath in the 1770s, and Elizabeth particularly had many admirers. Her father intended to make a profitable match for her, but she seems to have a gift for getting her own way in a charmingly melting manner and neatly persuaded her father's rich but elderly choice not only to withdraw his suit but to settle a large sum of his money on her as well, after which she eloped happily with Sheridan. Her sister, Maria, *(seated)* died very young— as indeed, not very much later, did Elizabeth herself. Gainsborough, who lived in Bath for 16 years, painted several portraits of Elizabeth as well as this one of both sisters. *(108)*

*Major Charles Davis (Left)*
In 1878 Charles Davis, Bath city engineer, was investigating a leak from the King's Bath. By then it was known that considerable Roman remains lay under the city, much careful work having been done by James Irvine, assistant to the architect Sir Gilbert Scott who was then working on the restoration of Bath Abbey. But now Major Davis found himself on the edge of a great discovery. His builder, Richard Mann—and a friend of James Irvine—had to tunnel along what turned out to be a great Roman overflow drain from the Roman reservoir *underneath* the King's Bath in order to pursue the municipal leak. So he came upon the massive walls of the Roman reservoir itself. Major Davis ordered the King's Bath drained and the floor removed; for the first time in 2,000 years the sacred spring was revealed. *(110)*

Sir Isaac Pitman *(Right)*—and he probably preferred to see his name neatly written in Pitman's Shorthand, which he invented in the early nineteenth century and first revealed in 1844 in a fourpenny booklet called *Stenographic Sound-Hand. (95)*

*By permission of the National Portrait Gallery.*

**Jane Austen** *(Left)*

Jane set her novel *Northanger Abbey* in Bath, and much of *Persuasion,* although she was never very fond of the city despite being a "desperate walker" and enjoying long walks in the surrounding countryside. She often visited it and her letters to her sister Cassandra, who made this sketch of her, are full of talk of food and bonnets and trimmings. In 1800 her father, the Reverend Austen, took a house in Sydney Place and later in Gay Street; he died there, and in 1806 Jane left Bath for good. But she must have been happy there once, because those years were crucial in her life. It was about this time that she fell in love, and something happened to put a tragic end to the affair. And although many of her comments about Bath are caustic, there is a passage in *Persuasion* that is not. Anne Elliott has often been identified with Jane herself, and there is one moment that must be a memory of her own brief happiness, when Anne at long last meets her lover Captain Wentworth in Union Street, just below Milsom Street.

" . . . they returned again into the past, more exquisitely happy, perhaps, in their reunion, than when it had first been projected; more tender, more tried, more fixed in a knowledge of each other's character, truth, and attachment; more equal to act, more justified in acting. And there, as they slowly paced the gradual ascent, heedless of every group around them, seeing neither sauntering politicians, bustling housekeepers, flirting girls, nor nursery-maids and children, they could indulge in those retrospections and acknowledgements, and especially in those explanations of what had directly preceded the present moment, which were so poignant and so ceaseless in interest. All the little variations of the last week were gone through; and of yesterday and today there could scarcely be an end." *(111)*

**The Sarah Siddons playbill** *(Right)*

The Theatre Royal belonged to the renowned Sarah Siddons, most celebrated of English tragic actresses, who appeared there with her husband and sister. The old Theatre Royal in Old Orchard Street, erected in 1750, (now the Masonic Hall), was managed by the celebrated John Palmer, MP, originator of the Mail Coach System and holder of the first Royal Patent ever granted to a provincial theatre. *(111A)*

---

## THEATRE-ROYAL, BATH.

This prefent THURSDAY, being the 17th of *January*, 1782,
Will be Perform'd a DRAMATIC POEM call'd

# ELFRIDA.

(Written by Mr. MASON.)
The MUSIC Compofed by Dr. ARNE.

Athelwold, Mr BROWNE.
Orgar, Mr BRUNTON.
Ardulph, Mr. ROWBOTHAM.
Edwin, Mr PAYNE.
Knights, Mr. G. SUMMERS, &c.
AND
Edgar, Mr. DIMOND.

Albina, Mifs SCRACE.
AND
Elfrida, Mrs. SIDDONS.
*Singing Virgins,* Mifs TWIST, Mifs WEWITZER, Mrs. BRETT,
Mrs DIDIER, Mrs. KEASBERRY, and Mrs. POWELL.

*To which will be added a* New Scotch PASTORAL OPERA call'd

# The Gentle Shepherd

(Alter'd from ALLAN RAMSAY by RICHARD TICKELL, Efq.)
As now Performing at the *Theatre-Royal,* in *Drury-Lane,* with Univerfal Applaufe.
The Overture and Accompaniments by Mr. LINLEY.—With new Scenery, Dreffes, &c.

| | | |
|---|---|---|
| Patie, Mr BRETT. | Sir William, Mr. BRUNTON. |
| Roger, Mr. BONNOR. | Jenny, Mifs WEWITZER. |
| Glaud, Mr PAYNE. | Maufe, Mrs KEASBERRY |
| Simon, Mr. JACKSON. | Madge, Mrs. SUMMERS. |
| Bauldy, Mr. BLISSET. | And Peggy, Mifs TWIST. |

The SONGS of the GENTLE SHEPHERD to be had at the different
Offices of the Theatre, and of the Fruit Woman.

☞ To begin precifely at SIX o'Clock.
Tickets and Places for the Boxes to be taken at the Box Lobby of the Theatre where Attendance will be
given from Ten to Two and from Three till Five. *Vivant Rex & Regina.*

Saturday the CHAPTER of ACCIDENTS, with the Pantomime of *Robinfon Crufoe.*

(*Right*) Rebirth of a waterway. *(112)*

# *Awakening*

The dream was over by the beginning of the 19th century. The people of Bath had for so long made a comfortable living out of well-heeled visitors that they found it hard to adjust to the fact that the elderly aunts and impoverished military gentlemen now not only visiting but retiring to the city could not afford the old lavish pleasures. There was a lot of piety about and a great many clergymen. That put a damper on things too. The only reference at the time to the red light district of Avon Street is to "the receptacle for unfortunate women." The fact was that Bath, more than most other cities, was having to face harsh economic reality

after the cushioning of the 18th century. It was simply not making things to make money. There was cloth manufacturing still at Twerton village, some brewing, and the stone quarries, but as Peter Egan said in his *Walks Around Bath* in 1819:

"The trade of Bath is, therefore, now confined exclusively to retail custom; and dependent entirely upon the caprice of fashion, or the mere home consumption of the City and its neighbourhood.

    Tradesmen! a set of vulgar swine,
    Crutches for a fortune in a deep
      decline . . .''

At the same time there were in Bath some 80 doctors of various kinds, ten dancing schools, 40 music teachers and innumerable lawyers. Not a good base for any economy.

It was hoped that the Kennet and Avon Canal, opened in 1810 to link London with Bath via Newbury and the Thames, would help matters, and for a time it did, providing a cheap export route for coal, timber, stone and other local produce. But it had taken a lot of time and money since its inception in 1794. Although the coalfields of North Somerset were doing well—there were collieries at Radstock, Midsomer Norton, Kilmersdon, and all over that

(*Above*) Widcombe Lock on the Kennet and Avon Canal. *(113)*

(*Right*) The Dundas Aqueduct – canal over river. *(114)*

*(Left)* The long pond at Widcombe. *(115)*

*(Below Left)* Painted narrow boat. *(116)*

*(Bottom Left)* The old malthouse. *(117)*

*(Bottom Right)* The old mill. *(118)*

part of otherwise rural countryside south of the city, and the last pit closed in the 1960s at Radstock—the railways were fast growing. In 1852 the Kennet and Avon company sold out to the Great Western Railway.

Ironically, the Kennet and Avon Canal is now one of Bath's success stories. Yet in 1955 the nationalised British Transport Commission applied to Parliament to abandon it. It had deteriorated rapidly in disuse. It was leaking. But a group of enthusiasts had already got together to save it. Parliament backed them. In 1961 the Kennet and Avon Trust was formed to restore the canal, and volunteers worked with untiring energy in mud and weeds and cement to open it for boats and swans and fishermen again. The Corporation helped to finance the restoration of Widcombe Locks. Today, from this first upward flight of locks from the river, you can follow the canal's airy swan-winged towpath out to Bathampton and beyond. On one hand graceful Regency and early Victorian houses step down to gardens from the green hill of Bath, and roses grow over the still water. On the other, the city hangs below and spreads to the haze of Bristol and the Welsh Hills. Tiny white fretworked bridges span the lilied meanders. They are cast iron, these bridges, and you can see a name on them: Stothert & Pitt. There were, in the early 19th century, just a few individuals who reckoned you could make money out of making things. One of them was an ironmonger called George Stothert who had set up his business in 1784.

By 1836 George Stothert had one son running an iron foundry and another building locomotives for the Great Western Railway. In 1844 Robert Pitt joined the company. They went into shipbuilding. By 1860 the firm was making all kinds of engineering products: and one was beginning to dominate. Cranes. Names like Titan,

(Above) Isambard Kingdom Brunel's
Bath Spa Station for the Great Western
Railway. (119)

(Left) Engine sheds at Green
Park – where the LMS (London
Midland & Scottish) met the S & D
(Somerset & Dorset). (120)

*(Left)* North Parade Bridge. *(121)*

Goliath and Mammoth became familiar all over the world. Today, almost every dockside from Murmansk to Sydney has a Stothert & Pitt crane. The firm makes winches, pumps, construction plant and heavy road making machinery, and although it now has a modern headquarters on the Lower Bristol Road in Bath, its old factory remains one of the dark satanic mills on the river.

Cranes of a different kind are the trademark of another Bath company, Sparrows. These are mobile cranes, developed since the last war when George Sparrow built a couple of two ton cranes out of old gun tractors and hired them out for laying gas pipes. His three sons went further and developed specialised powered cranes which Sparrows now hire all over the world, lifting as much as a thousand tons at a time.

Specialisation has become a characteristic of Bath industries. Inventiveness, too. In 1879 Gustav Horstmann, a clockmaker who had married a Bath girl in 1848 and settled in the city, had already perfected a perpetual self-winding clock. In 1904 his four sons set up in business to make a patent gear and called themselves the Horstmann Gear Company. Today, it is the Horstmann Gear Group, with subsidiaries in Wales and Australia, and has become one of the leaders of high technology precision engineering. The chairman is still a Horstmann, and many other members of the family are

still part of the company: the headquarters flourishes at Newbridge, where they were making munitions for the war effort in 1916.

More recently, in 1956, Jeremy Fry started working on an idea for developing a valve actuator. His workshop was in the basement of his home at Widcombe Manor. Valves have regulated the flow of gases or liquids in pipelines since Roman times, but today a man cannot even reach a valve somewhere in a great processing plant, a refinery, under the sea or out in the desert. Jeremy Fry's actuators solved the problem. He founded Rotork, one of the engineering success stories of the 1960s and now consolidating its position all over the world, although the firm's headquarters is still on the Upper Bristol Road in a suitably immaculately designed building on the river.

Pitman's Printing Works is across the river on the Lower Bristol Road. It was founded by Isaac Pitman, another Bath inventor. His invention is used by millions of secretaries: Pitman's shorthand. It was in 1844 that he wrote a little fourpenny book called *Stenographic Sound-Hand*. He was also something of a fanatic about phonetic spelling, and his first printing works was called "Fonetic Instituweon and Printing Ofis". He was knighted for his work on shorthand and spelling but it is perhaps not surprising that his reformed alphabet never caught on. His great-grandson, however, Sir James Pitman, invented the Initial

Teaching Alphabet, or i.t.a., which is still used in schools.

Cabinet-making has long been a local industry, but brought well into the 20th century by such firms as Herman Miller and Arkana, also along the Bristol Road.

So, gradually, Bath changed again. Isambard Kingdom Brunel brought the Great Western Railway and built his crenellated Spa Station, and in 1869 the Midland Railway came to the city and linked up with the beautiful old Somerset and Dorset Line with its long tunnel up to Combe Down, sadly closed in 1966. New bridges crossed the Avon: North Parade Bridge in 1835, the Cleveland Bridge in 1827. The Victorians capitalised on Bath's architectural reputation by doing quite a lot to despoil it, but they also built some fine Italianate villas on Bathwick Hill and elsewhere, and much of their work is now seen to be handsome and fitting. Sir Gilbert Scott spent 10 years lovingly restoring Bath Abbey and working on its great fan vaulted roof.

In the 1880s Spas were in fashion again and people came back to try the hot mineral waters for the sake of their livers and lumbago: the city engineer, investigating a leak from the King's Bath, made the first discovery of the Roman baths. At last that ancient achievement was revealed again, if rather heavily ornamented by Victorian statues and balustrades, and just at the right time to tap the new enthusiasm for antiquities.

*(Left)* Cleveland Bridge. *(122)*

(*Top*) Award-winning new factory for Herman Miller, furniture makers. *(123)*

(*Above*) North Sea gas comes ashore controlled by Rotork valve actuators – success story for Bath industry. *(124)*

(*Left*) One of Sparrows' cranes doing a bit of delicate work at the Royal Crescent. *(126)*

(Left) Stothert & Pitt cranes – just a few of the 42 on the dockside in Jeddah, Saudi Arabia. (127)

(Below Left) One of Stothert & Pitt's earlier giants – the 50-ton travelling Titan crane. (128)

(Bottom) A Horstmann time-switch extensively used throughout the UK in domestic central heating systems (129)

(Below Right) Modern lithographic printing for the 1980s by Dawson & Goodall. (130)

By the beginning of the 20th century, some people were becoming concerned that Bath was altering a little too much. In 1909 a Trust was formed which is now the Bath Preservation Trust, and one of its early achievements was to awaken the Corporation's conscience so that it brought in an Act in 1925 to ensure that all new building in Bath should be either of real Bath Stone or artificial facsimile.

In 1942 there was an alteration that no one could escape: there were three bombing raids within two nights, and 400 people died. The Assembly Rooms, among much else, were destroyed. Today they have been meticulously restored—and the chandeliers, which had prudently been put in store at the outbreak of the war, are resplendently original.

It was the last war, too, which made the Admiralty decamp from London to Bath, and thus produce a new influx of some 8,000 people with red brick encampments on the edges of the city. They took over the Empire Hotel, that gabled Victorian monument to the materialistic spirit of the age that stands opposite the Abbey in the Orange Grove. But gradually, although they did not return to London after the war, but stayed, the civil servants were assimilated into the life of the city. So have the students of the new Bath University, established with considerable opposition in 1964, when it emerged out of Bristol College of Advanced Technology and was founded up on Claverton Down. And so, too, have new ways of life and new buildings. Like some elderly but still beautiful and sharp-witted woman, Bath has adjusted her stays, taken a hard look at herself in the mirror and decided to make the best of old age. She can still dream: but all of us have to face reality.

Bath Blitz, 1942

*(Above)* Destruction of the Francis Hotel, Queen Square *(131)*

*(Left)* What was left of the Assembly Rooms *(132)*

*(Above)* Bath University. *(133)*

*(Right)* Bath University degree
ceremony. *(134)*

# Daydreaming

Bath is eminently suitable for daydreaming in. It has in fact been said that Bath has the kind of slumbrous climate that makes it rather difficult to do anything else. It makes the most mundane of shopping expeditions into an excuse for lingering. You find yourself hesitating on a corner to look up at Bathwick and the lights coming on in the dusk, or at Beechen Cliff, shadowy and oddly intangible against a summer noon sky. It is therefore a wise precaution to allow more than sufficient time for actually buying things, even if you intend only to buy a packet of teabags and the washing powder you forgot last time. Shopping itself is a procedure fraught with temptation, since Bath is one of the finest shopping centres in Britain.

This is not to say that it has bigger department stores or more shops than anywhere else: it has not. It simply has more good shops than most other provincial cities, more idiosyncratic shops, more interesting shops. As in Wood's day, it divides roughly into Upper and Lower parts, the Upper including that provincial Bond Street, Milsom Street—and indeed Bath's own New Bond Street too—and a great many small streets, paved alleyways, corridors and markets all north of the spacious expanse of Abbey Churchyard which is itself crammed with good shops. In the Lower Town is the modern Southgate shopping precinct with Marks and Spencer's, Woolworth's, Boots and Littlewoods, neatly combined with such traditional and well-established local emporiums as William Mitchell's, drapers. Walcot is a shade more raffish, with secondhand shops, bicycles, secondhand furniture and antiques. The most essentially tempting thing about the whole lot is that they are all so close together. Bath is a pedestrian city. You can walk from top to bottom in about 20 minutes, except that no one ever does because it is so easy to get sidetracked: you can wander down cobbled streets, under stone archways, into covered markets, and always find yourself with a glimpse of a green hill or the Abbey or the river. In fact Bath is not a motorists' city. Local inhabitants have been known to go grey trying to park and visitors have been known to give up altogether.

Music has always been a good reason for daydreaming in Bath, whether you sit in Sydney Gardens listening to the band, in the Pump Room drinking coffee to the music of the Pump Room Trio, or in the Abbey at Evensong. And if you are serious about music, there is the Bath Festival, which has become an established and international musical event since the first one in 1948.

*(Opposite)* Daydreaming in the Royal Crescent *(135)*

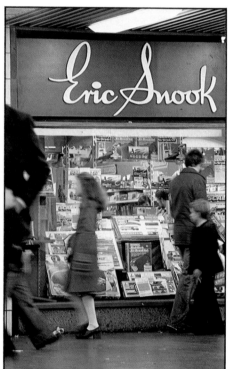

Shopping in Bath, "a procedure fraught with temptation", since the city is one of the finest shopping centres in Britain. *(136-150)*

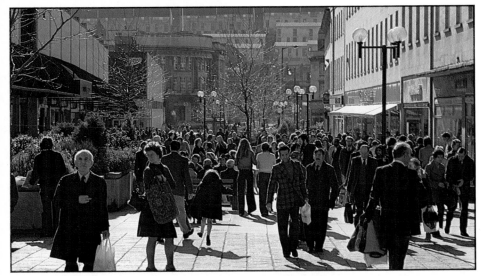

*(Opposite)* The Lindsay String Quartet in the Guildhall at the 1978 Bath Festival. *(151)*

*(Right)* Tea and Bath Buns in the Pump Room. *(152)*

There is cricket in the summer, often with Somerset playing, and you can sit in the sun to the sound of leather on willow. And football and rugby in the winter. Endless fishing, all the year round, fly fishing and coarse fishing. You can outwit a pike if you are lucky at Bathampton Weir. All along the river and the Kennet and Avon Canal, small boys sit with rods poised, sandwich boxes and tins full of squirming maggots. It is a curious thing that angling is somehow a very male pursuit. Little girls do not fish. Mothers wonder as they look at their offspring, suddenly so mysteriously and unnaturally immobile. Why is it that otherwise they are incapable of keeping still? Girlfriends, in the first flush of devotion, shiver in silence on riverbanks and meekly submit to being told to shut up or they'll frighten the fish. But wives get cynical, and just pack the sandwich boxes and declare that at least it keeps the men out of their way.

There is still a theatre in Bath, of course. The Theatre Royal is red plush, comfortable (unless you get behind a pillar) and charmingly intimate. As well as new cinemas there is the Little Theatre tucked behind the Hot Bath, where you can see old films. And there are restaurants everywhere, from the hamburger-with-baked-potato-with-cream-cheese-and-chives-and-relish sort

to the kind where you start by drinking sherry in a puce and celadon green sitting room with stuffed olives and *Country Life* on the coffee table. There are Italian ones where the waiters talk a lot, and French ones where they talk even more but among themselves so that the food, although very good, takes a long time to arrive. There is more than one good fish and chip shop and at Evans in Abbey Green you can have cod and chips twice in a Georgian dining room. Teashops abound where you can eat chocolate mikadoes, Bath Buns and Sally Lunn cakes dripping with butter. Wine bars cater for the young executives of the city and there are even some discreet Tandoori and Chinese restaurants if you look.

Bath has always excelled in the number of butchers, and if you search around in places like Bath Market you can find Bath Chaps, which are pigs' cheeks cooked and rolled (why?) into breadcrumbed giant cones. New and secondhand bookshops are scattered throughout the city, like antique shops: there are more and more good small art galleries and print shops too.

If shopping palls on wet days, or you happen to be broke, there are Museums. Bath has an unconscionable lot of them. At No. 1, Royal Crescent, courteous volunteer ladies of the Bath Preservation Trust which restored this

exquisite building welcome you into the authentically recreated rooms of a Georgian house. Bath Carriage Museum is more homely, smelling of the horses which now trot round the Circus pulling delighted visitors in carriages. The stables which house the Museum were built by John Wood.

The Holburne of Menstrie Museum, built by Charles Harcourt Masters in the early 19th century as a final swag of elegance at the end of Great Pulteney Street, is not visited enough because you have to walk rather further than usual in Bath to get to it, Pulteney Street being 1,100 feet long. But it is worth the effort, since it contains a feast of beautiful things, from paintings by Stubbs and Gainsborough to fine glass and porcelain. It also has a permanent study centre for contemporary craftsmanship of today.

Small girls of all ages enjoy the Museum of Costume at the Assembly Rooms, and small boys equally like the Camden Works Museum in Morford Street, which is a bit out of the way north of the Assembly Rooms. It is a complete recreation of the old brass foundry, engineering works, mineral water factory, shop and office founded by J. B. Bowler in Victorian times: you itch to start the machines clacking and bubbling again—as most of them are capable of doing.

*(Left)* Bath Sports and Leisure Centre. (153)

*(Below)* Judo at the Sports Centre. *(154)*

*(Above)* Cricket on Bath Recreation Ground in summer. *(155)*

*(Left)* Flat racing on Lansdown. *(156)*

(Above) Bath Rugby Club XV in action. (157)

(Left) Football at Twerton Park. (158)

(Left) Bowls in Victoria Park. (159)

(Above) Canoeing on Pulteney Weir. (160)

Small and beautiful, the Theatre Royal.
*(Top)* The actors' view. *(161)*
*(Below)* The stage itself. *(162)*

(Left) Evoking the past – carriage rides along Royal Crescent. (163)

(Right) Chiffon dress of c 1907 at the Museum of Costume. (164)

(Below) The Stencilled Bedroom at the American Museum; walls painted by a journeyman artist in about 1830 in exchange for board and lodging and a modest fee. (165)

Above the Reference Library in Queen Square is Bath Geology Museum where you can find out about that rather unsung Father of Geology, William Smith, and at George Bayntun's in Manvers Street near the railway station you can see what bookbinding is all about. There is a Toy Museum too, in York Street.

Up on Claverton Down is the American Museum, founded by two Americans who thought English people might like to know more about their American history. The American Museum is directed by Ian McCallum, who from the beginning in 1959 worked closely with the founders. Churchill made his first political speech in this beautiful early 19th century manor, and it is now a place in which to spend all

afternoon, enjoying not only the perfect and authentic interiors of early American homes but the spectacular views of the Limpley Stoke valley, the beautiful gardens and one of the best afternoon teas you can get anywhere.

And, of course, there is the Roman Baths Museum. Try to see the Museum and the Roman Baths when there are few people about, so that you can imagine how it must have been, crowded, steamy, under a great shadowy stone roof, smelling of hot oil, echoing with voices.

Bath has its own countryside, too. There are parks like friendly, open Royal Victoria, with the Royal Crescent smiling on it, and children's lakes, and avenues of cherry blossom, rare trees in the Botanic Gardens and circuses and

hot air balloons and fairs in summer. Hidden parks like Henrietta, where there is a scented garden for the blind—and a dog toilet; high parks like Alexandra, from which you can look out northward over the whole city, and little secret parks like Alice. Here and there are tucked bits of real countryside, like the snug farm folded behind the green curve of Bathwick Hill, where in winter children toboggan perilously down towards Sydney Buildings and the canal. You can climb Lansdown and walk at Mount Beacon, that backwater which twines around an escarpment and gives one of the finest views of Bath. Weston is still villagey, and Perrymead, off Ralph Allen's Drive, turns into open fields and woods: Widcombe is like a Tuscan hamlet with a dovecotted farm,

(*Left*) Rare trees and plants in the Botanic Gardens, Victoria Park. *(166)*

(*Below*) Shades of Tuscany – Widcombe Village and Manor. *(167)*

(*Above opposite*) Farleigh Castle, Farleigh Hungerford, overlooking the valley of the Frome. *(168)*

(*Below opposite*) The George Inn, Norton St Philip, from whose mediaeval balcony the notorious Judge Jefferies sentenced the rebel followers of the Duke of Monmouth to hang, in the 17th century. *(169)*

Thomas à Becket church and a golden manor house.

Further afield, the setting for Bath, are the stony cosy Cotswolds to the north and snug Somerset to the south, with villages like Norton St. Philip where Judge Jefferies sentenced men to hang from the gallery of the George Inn in the 17th century, and Farleigh Hungerford, where a ruined castle nests above a winding wooded valley of the Frome, and you can see herons. Eastward is plump expansive Wiltshire with wool towns like Bradford-on-Avon, which gave its name to that other Bradford in Yorkshire, and villages like Lacock, half timbered and thatched. West is Bristol, that seaport scarred by slavery, unrepentant, crowded, industrial, musical, vigorous.

And here at the heart of it all, incongruous and on a wet day even faintly absurd, so bedraggled can it look, is this Italianate confection, a honey, grey and amber little city first built upon the dreams of men who longed for the sun of Rome. So did John Wood dream of his Palladian city. We all have our own remote arcadian dreams, and Bath, of all things built by men, can seem as close as it is possible to get.

I used to run out of school at ten to four, and down Lansdown with like-minded friends, and sometimes, in that hazy sun of endless afternoons, we used to be aware that Bath was a lovely place to live. We did not say so, but we felt it then. Nor have we changed.

(*Previous recto and verso pages*) Aerial view of the City. *(170)*

# Bibliography

Apart from talking to the people of Bath I also read works by Jane Austen, Smollett, Christopher Anstey and other contemporary writers. The staff of Bath museums, especially Jill Knight of the Victoria Art Gallery, and Bath reference library assistants, were very helpful. I also read the following books:

BRABAZON, A. B., *Bath Mineral Waters* (1978)
CECIL, David, *Portrait of Jane Austen* (1978)
CUNLIFFE, Barry, *Roman Bath Discovered* (1971)
EGAN, Peter, *Walks Through Bath* (1819)
FREEMAN, Jean, *Jane Austen in Bath* (1969)
HADDON, John, *Bath* (1973)
ISON, Walter, *The Georgian Buildings of Bath* (1948)
KERSLEY, George, *Bath Water* (1973)
PANTER, Helen, *Edgar* (1972)
PEACH, R. E., *Historic Houses in Bath* (1883)
PERKINS BROOKS & PEARCE, *Bath Stone—A Quarry History* (1979)
PICKFORD, R., *William Smith* (1977)
SITWELL, Edith, *Bath* (1932)
SMITH, R. A. L., *Bath* (1944)
SMITHSON, Peter, *Bath* (1971)
TREVELYAN, G. M., *English Social History* (1944)
TUNSTALL, Dr., *Rambles About Bath* (1889)

D. W.

# Photographic Acknowledgments

(In the text the picture reference numbers are shown in parenthesis.)

Her Majesty the Queen—*98*

The National Portrait Gallery—*86, 87, 93, 100, 101, 107, 111*
The Governors of Dulwich Picture Gallery—*108*
The B.B.C. Hulton Picture Library—*7, 84*
The Geological Society of London—*96*
The Royal National Hospital for Rheumatic Diseases—*89A*
The Holburne of Menstrie Museum—*34, 42, 105*
The Trustees of the Theatre Royal, Bath—*161, 162*
Ivo Peters, Esq.—*120*
The Archives of Bath City Council—*8, 9, 20, 37, 38, 39, 40, 41, 45, 71, 76, 77, 78, 85, 102, 109, 151*
Brian Davis, Esq. (Bath City Council)—*24, 27, 46, 47, 67, 75, 149, 167*

Bath Reference Library—*29, 90, 91, 110*
The Photographic Department, University of Bath—*1, 74, 133*
The American Museum—*165*
Bath Museums Service—*8, 102, 111A, 164*
Bath & Portland Group—*1B*
Dawson & Goodall—*130*
Horstmann Gear Group—*129*
Herman Miller—*123*
Pitman Press—*95*
Rotork Engineering—*125*
Sparrows—*126*
Stothert & Pitt—*127, 128*
Graham Harrison—*2, 10A, 15, 19, 21, 23, 31, 32, 50, 51, 56, 58, 60, 64, 68, 69, 70, 80, 81, 83, 88, 89, 92, 94, 97, 99, 103, 104, 106, 114, 135, 136, 137, 138, 139, 140, 141, 142, 143, 146, 147, 148, 150, 152, 163, 168, 169*

John Betteridge—*4, 5, 20, 26, 26A, 28, 34, 37, 38, 39, 40, 41, 42, 45, 49, 52, 54, 55, 61, 63, 71, 76, 77, 78, 79, 82, 109, 130, 145*
Frans and Heather Vahrmeyer (Unichrome)—*3, 6, 10B, 11, 12, 13, 14, 16, 17, 18, 30, 59, 62, 65, 72, 144, 166, 170*
Dr. Leslie Bowcock—*25, 33, 48, 57, 66, 112, 115, 116, 117, 118, 134, 153*
Bath Evening Chronicle—*122, 131, 132, 154, 155, 156, 157, 158, 159, 160*
Robert Axten—*22, 35, 44, 113, 119, 121*

Bath, England,
with Priscilla,
Sept. 13, 1984

# The
# Dream
# of
# Bath

Other books by Diana Winsor

*Published by Macmillan:*
Red on Wight, *a thriller* (1972)
The Death Convention (1974)